Navigating True North

MY JOURNEY FROM BLIND FAITH TO BOLD FAITH

by

Natalie Dee Latzka, JD

Navigating True North: My Journey from Blind Faith to Bold Faith
Copyright © 2021 by Natalie Dee Latzka

Published by Deep River Books
Sisters, Oregon
www.deepriverbooks.com

All rights reserved. No part of this book may be reproduced or transmitted in any form or by any means, electronic or mechanical, including photocopying and recording, or by any information storage and retrieval system, without permission in writing from the publisher.

All Scripture is taken from the THE HOLY BIBLE, NEW INTERNATIONAL VERSION®, NIV® Copyright © 1973, 1978, 1984, 2011 by Biblica, Inc.® Used by permission. All rights reserved worldwide.

Cover design by Robin Black, Inspirio Design

ISBN—13: 9781632695581
Library of Congress Control Number: 2021902175

Printed in the USA
2021—First Edition
29 28 27 26 25 24 23 22 21 10 9 8 7 6 5 4 3 2 1

Dedicated to my three beautiful babies:
Haley, Allison, and Megan.

May you always have the strength and
courage to STAND, and be blessed with the
grace and opportunity to CLIMB.

TABLE OF CONTENTS

PART I

LOST

Chapter 1

TRUE VS. MAGNETIC NORTH

"*Not all those who wander are lost.*" This well-known line from a poem in J. R. R. Tolkien's epic story *The Lord of the Rings* was intended to describe the character Aragorn. Aragorn is a ranger whose job is to patrol the northern boundaries of Middle-earth to protect the region from evil forces. While many consider him nothing more than a vagabond aimlessly roaming lost through the wilderness, others recognize that his journeys are preparing him to ultimately fulfill his destiny. The time he spends wandering in the wilderness provides him the insight to not only discover who he is, but unsuspectingly positions him to take his rightful place as King of Gondor. Aragorn may have been a wanderer, but he certainly was not lost.

I would also describe myself as a bit of a wanderer. In fact, I have the Tolkien quote prominently displayed on the back of my Jeep to identify me as such. One of my very favorite things in the whole world is to spend time wandering in the mountains. I can be hiking on foot or driving in the jeep, it doesn't matter. Typically, I set out with no purpose other than to find the perfect spot where I can sit and just be. I am never sure where my wandering will lead me, but I always seem to reach my intended destination. The breathtaking beauty of the mountains and the nature that surrounds me give me the greatest sense of peace I have ever known. Unlike Aragorn, however, I have on occasion found myself *very* lost!

There is a distinct difference between wandering and being lost. My personal definition of "wandering" is: setting out on a journey to explore without the need to establish a destination or the pressure of being on a timeline. My definition of "lost," on the other hand, is: not knowing where you are or how to get back to where you need to be.

When hiking in the mountains, a wise wanderer is always prepared in the event she finds herself lost. Today, most hikers are equipped with GPS devices. Those handy things will get you pointed in the right direction in no time—unless, of course, there is heavy cloud cover blocking the satellite signal or your battery is not fully charged. In that case you'd better hope you have an old-fashioned compass hidden away in your backpack for emergencies. Unfortunately, even a compass can fail you. If you are unfamiliar with how it works, it can actually get you pointed in the wrong direction. Let me give you a quick scenario to illustrate.

Billy Backpacker and his friends decided they wanted to hike up to a remote little lake in the mountains to camp for a couple days. Before they set out, they talked to a ranger to get more information about the area. The ranger warned them that there was some bad weather expected in the next couple days. He told them that if they experienced any problems, they should take shelter at the ranger station about a mile due north of the lake. Billy and the gang headed off to the lake. Everything was great until the following day when they heard some thunder off in the distance and noticed some nasty clouds rolling in. To play it safe, they decided to head to the ranger station to take cover. Because of the storm, Billy's GPS was not getting a signal; luckily, he had his trusty compass tucked away in his backpack. He oriented his compass to north and he and the group took off for the ranger station. Unfortunately, the group never made it to the ranger station; in fact, they ended up quite lost in the middle of a bad mountain storm. What Billy didn't realize was that the ranger station was in a *true* north direction from the lake and that his compass was leading them in the direction of *magnetic* north. There is a difference.

There are actually two different directional locations for north. One is magnetic north and the other is true north. Magnetic north is a point on the earth's surface where the planet's magnetic field points vertically downward. Scientists believe it is caused by rivers of molten metal at the earth's core which generate electrical currents. Since a compass needle is essentially just a little magnet, it will point in the direction of the earth's magnetic field. This direction is referred to as magnetic north.

The second northerly direction is known as true north. To get a good understanding of where true north is located, take a look at a globe. True north is the point at which all the longitude lines meet at the very top of the globe. It would also theoretically mark the location of the earth's imaginary rotational axis, on which it turns 360 degrees every twenty-four hours. At night, the direction of true north can be located by using the North Star, which is the brightest star at the end of the Little Dipper's handle.

What most people do not realize is that magnetic north and true north lie in two different directions. If you are curious and want to see the difference between the two, try this little experiment: Locate the North Star in the sky, and at the same time locate the direction of north on a compass. You will see they point you in slightly different directions, the angle of which depends on where you are located on the earth's surface. As of 2019, the physical distance between the point of magnetic north and true north was about 310 miles.[1]

The really interesting thing is that the location of magnetic north actually changes over time. As the earth rotates around the sun the rivers of metal flow which causes the earth's magnetic pole to shift. To give you some perspective of how magnetic north can change over time, here are a few statistics. In 2009, geological surveys positioned magnetic north in the Canadian Arctic. Ten years later, in 2019, magnetic north is located very close to Siberia, Russia.[2] Scientists estimate that magnetic north moves as much as thirty miles per year.[3]

Because true north never changes, most navigational maps and directions are oriented to true north. Therefore, if you use your compass to navigate to a location based on true north coordinates, you will not make it to your intended destination. This does not mean you should get up and immediately throw your compass in the garbage; a compass can be a very useful tool. My main point is this: if you are going to rely on a compass for direction, you need to understand how it works.

I have found myself lost in the mountains on more than one occasion. Fortunately (knock on wood) I have always been able to find my way safely back to where I needed to be. Unfortunately, being lost in the mountains is not my only experience with being lost. I have also found myself in the position of being utterly and hopelessly lost as I wandered through life. I had always considered myself fairly well prepared for possible challenges life could throw my way. I had been raised a Christian; I was a good person, followed the rules, said my prayers, and most importantly I had "faith" in God. I guess you could say I considered faith to be my compass. I believed it would help keep me safely pointed in the right direction. It turns out that was not the case.

When a series of challenging life events knocked me off course, I relied on my faith compass for direction. Like Billy Backpacker, my compass just seemed to take me further and further off course. No matter how hard I tried I could not seem to get back on track. I soon realized that being lost in life felt just about as terrifying as being lost in the mountains.

I was at a complete loss. According to everything I had been taught I was going in the right direction. I had a successful career, family, and faith in God. How could I be so completely lost? Desperate to find a sense of direction I prayed for God's guidance and clung to Bible verses I had learned when I was young: "But those who hope in the LORD will renew their strength. They will soar on wings like eagles; they will run and not grow weary, they will walk and not be faint" (Isaiah 40:31); "Trust the LORD with all your heart and lean not on your own understanding; in all your ways submit to him and he will make your paths straight" (Proverbs

3:5-6). Unfortunately, things just continued to go from bad to worse. Eventually I found myself lost at the bottom a very deep pit and I had no clue how to get out. Somehow my faith compass had failed me—and even more disheartening was the fact that God had failed me.

Let me tell you a bit more about myself. It might help give you a little more context concerning this faith crisis I found myself in. As I reflect back, I realize I was far from perfect. To be honest, on many occasions I was what you might call a hot mess. Despite that, I was a good person, I worked hard, and I truly believed in God. He was supposed to help believers like me out of these bad spots and make us better than who we were—at least that is what I was told.

I'm going to share my story with you, knowing it makes me vulnerable to criticism and others' judgment. I share my story because my experience with faith is likely one that others struggle with as well. I share it as an example of how, despite best efforts to live the right way, you can still end up lost. Lastly, I share my story so that if you are feeling lost in life, you know that you are not alone.

As I share my story, I am going to call out certain events and decisions that I call "WTF moments." By the way, "WTF" stands for "where things failed." I know that it's also an acronym representing a fairly inappropriate expression of dismay, so forgive me if you find it offensive. It has just become a fairly accurate and satisfying way to express how I feel about my past failures. I share my WTF moments with you because they are good examples of how bad decisions can knock us off track and contribute to getting us lost. Most importantly, I point them out so that if you are finding yourself in a similar situation you take all efforts to prevent those WTF moments before they happen!

Get comfy and buckle in—it is a long and bumpy story!

Chapter 2

MY STORY

If I were to give you the social media version of my story, it wouldn't sound so bad. Check it out: My name is Natalie Latzka, I am an attorney, and I worked for a multimillion-dollar corporation for twenty-four-plus years. I have three amazing and beautiful daughters and have an incredibly supportive family and wonderful friends. I have stood on the summit of some of the world's most amazing mountains, have been fortunate enough to travel around the world, and have experienced adventure most people only dream of. Basically, I have it all: career, family, pension, retirement fund, and a beautiful house in the burbs. #AmericanDream

As is typical with social media versions of the story, minor details have been excluded. Let me tell you a little bit more about my story—the parts you *don't* normally see on social media: My name is Natalie Latzka. I have been divorced, bankrupt, used, and dumped. At times, I have been a crappy mom, sister, daughter, and friend. I swear like a drunken sailor and occasionally drink more than I should. I have acted like a holier-than-thou Christian one minute, and the next have doubted the very existence of God. Despite having tried to live my life the "right way," I feel like I have spent a good deal of it lost without direction. I am tired, angry, bitter, and beat-up. #LoseBomb

(Note: This is a good reminder for those of us who look with envy on the lives others present in social media. Know that there is always more to the story!)

My Childhood

I would start out by telling you some fun and interesting stories about my childhood, but the fact is, I don't remember much. I grew up in the 1970s in a fairly middle-class family in central Minnesota with two younger brothers. Overall, I would say my brothers and I had a pretty good childhood. We always had what we needed and without a doubt knew we were loved.

Like any family, mine had its challenges. I will cut to the chase and give you the lowdown on where my family struggled. My parents were extreme opposites. They communicated differently, they loved differently, and ultimately had different philosophies about life. I do remember times when we all laughed and had fun together as a family. What I remember most, however, are the times the laughter and fun were abruptly interrupted by what I will refer to as unpredictable emotional chaos. From my humble perspective, I would say the cause of that chaos was the extreme differences between my parents. Their differences would lead to conflict which typically escalated into heated arguments, eventually exploding into uncontrolled, emotional chaos.

I don't say this to blame or shame anyone. I love both my mom and dad deeply. I tell you this because we all experience challenges in childhood that can have a profound impact on who we become. I am sure all of you have experienced pain and challenges in your childhood as well. I can tell you that for me, identifying and acknowledging them have been an important part of leaving them behind. If you find yourself struggling to make sense of the past, I strongly encourage you to find help to sort through it.

I would also like to take some time to talk about the religious aspects of my childhood. I very purposefully use the word "religious" to describe my spiritual experiences as a child. My recollection is that much of my religious experience was focused on ritualism and "following the rules." I was raised Catholic. To be honest, I found my religious education to be, for lack of a better word, confusing. I was taught that God was loving and just, but angry and harsh to those who disobeyed him. I was taught that God was our Father and loved each of us personally, but he also seemed to require a great deal of ceremonial reverence. I grew up believing that faith could "move mountains," but that success was somehow conditional on your level of faith and how diligently you followed the rules. Again, I do not share these things to blame or shame Catholicism or any religion. I acknowledge that what I was taught was based on what others sincerely believed and presented with the best of intentions.

As mentioned earlier, I do not recall many details from my childhood. I do, however, have one very vivid memory: for as long as I can remember I have had an extreme need to find purpose, meaning, and significance in my life. I mention this because it has been an ever-present force in my life, and I suspect it has been an underlying motivation for many of the choices I have made as I have wandered through life.

Young Adulthood

As a kid I had always been painfully shy, but as I moved into my college years that changed a little. I gained some self-confidence by working some very nontraditional jobs, especially for a girl: school bus driver, loss prevention officer, campus security officer, and police cadet. Forgive my crude language, but I was kind of a badass—at least for a girl! I found success with my new tough-girl persona and figured I could leverage that going forward to give me a little extra edge. I would probably have to say that this is one of those WTF moments I mentioned earlier. Being a tough guy (or gal, as the case may be) has its benefits. It can give you confidence to take some risks and, as they say, "walk the road less traveled." On the other hand, being tough can often be just a disguise to cover up the fear and insecurity that actually hides inside of us. It is important to know the difference.

By the spring of 1988, I had graduated from college with a bachelor of science in criminal justice and had just been accepted into law school. Life, as they say, seemed to be falling into place. There was just one thing that kept knocking me off-balance: despite the fact my hard work seemed to be putting me on the right trajectory for success, I was not finding the sense of purpose, meaning, and significance I was hoping for. Because I could not find it, I constantly felt, for lack of a better word, lost. I prayed and had faith that God would help me find my way.

I was quickly convinced that "love" was the missing piece of the equation. If I could find love, and someone to share my life with, I would certainly find the purpose, meaning, and significance I was in search of. As luck would have it, I was able to find the love of my life in no time at all! He was a really great guy and we had a really great relationship—well, most of the time anyway. To be honest, there were some pretty obvious warning signs very early on in our relationship. I chose to ignore them, or at the very least thought things would change once we were married and living happily ever after.

I am sure I am stating the obvious when I say this was a major WTF moment in my life. Just a word of advice for those of you currently considering a long-term committed relationship: if you are questioning your relationship because of differences in the way you think, how you treat each other, and how you handle life, be concerned! These are red flags. If I can give you one piece of advice it is this: don't ignore red flags! Take the time to acknowledge them and consider how those red-flag concerns will impact your future, because they will. If you are questioning whether or not your relationship with your special someone is throwing off any red flags, ask your friends and family—they will know.

Over the course of the next several years I put my head down and worked hard to accomplish my goals and establish what I thought would be a good foundation for a successful life. After graduating from law school, I passed the bar exam, got married, and was hired by a law firm as an associate attorney all in the span of about six months. And talk about bad girl: I was the first female attorney in the firm's seventy-five-year history.

While that sounds rather impressive from an outside perspective, let me give you a little of the inside reality of how awesome that really was . . . *not*! I was essentially a twenty-four-year-old little puppy, in a hierarchical pack of men between the ages of thirty-something and seventy-something. It quickly became apparent that none of them had the time or patience to answer questions from a clueless little "legally blonde" girl. I once asked if it would be OK to take on a client who desperately needed help but couldn't afford the retainer deposit. I was advised as follows, "You never take a case without a retainer unless it's a woman with big boobs and long legs; that woman has neither." I guess that answered that question. I also never really found the answer "justice will prevail" particularly helpful when asking for advice on how to handle an upcoming court appearance. I hated practicing law!

My plans for the perfect life were not working out so well. About the same time I quit my job, it had become fairly apparent that my marriage was in trouble as well. Looking back, it is very clear that we were both too immature and totally unprepared to deal with the life we had jumped into. A year into my textbook life, my husband and I went our separate ways and I moved back home with my mom and dad. I decided to go back to school and work toward a master's degree in political science. School was a happy and safe place for me (which I know makes me a big nerd!). During this time, I also very actively attempted to rejuvenate and renew my faith. I prayed constantly for direction and that God would help me find the purpose, meaning, and significance of my life I so craved.

My husband and I were separated for about a year when we decided to give things another try. I remember being very motivated to do the "right thing"; divorce was totally unacceptable in my world. Things were up and down, but we made it work. Before you knew it, we had three beautiful daughters and a sweet house in the burbs, and I had a promising corporate career. I presumably had everything I had ever wanted—except for one thing.

To my complete dismay, I continued to feel very lost. I was doing everything I was supposed to be doing. I worked hard, took care of my family, said my prayers, had faith in God, took my kids to Sunday school, and went to church. I could not figure out what the heck was wrong. The only thing I could determine was that I needed to do more. I doubled down on the prayers, committed to having even greater faith in God, and worked even harder. After all, "God helps those who help themselves," right?

In hindsight, this may not have been the right course of action. What actually happened was that my desire to find something "more" turned into an out-of-control obsession. It pushed me randomly and recklessly to manufacture ways to find some sense of purpose, meaning, and significance in my life. At one point, I decided to start my own side business, thinking that would certainly do the trick. My custom handmade greeting cards were designed to deliver special messages of encouragement to those who were hurting.

My card business was definitely a WTF moment in my life! Seriously, what was I thinking? Starting a side business in addition to working and managing a household with three kids was plain crazy. As you might imagine, that business venture did not last long.

If there is anything I have learned from all my WTF moments, it is that you can never find a sense of inner peace, contentment, joy, purpose, meaning, or significance by looking for it in the world around you. It can only be found on the inside. It took me a very long time to learn that lesson—so in the meantime I continued to look for it in the world.

I decided that a hobby could add some needed meaning to my life and would certainly be much more conducive to my schedule. I settled on mountain climbing! That would certainly give me the opportunity to see what I was made of and would be a great way to reconnect with my bad-girl persona, which had taken quite a hit over the past couple years. My dad and uncle were trekkers; I could join forces with them.

My new and improved life goal was to bag as many 14ers as possible. (In mountain-speak, that meant climbing peaks over 14,000 feet in elevation.) Within just a few short years I had trekked to the summits of the three tallest mountains in the continental United States and I loved it! Finally, I had found something that touched my soul and helped me find a profound sense of inner peace and clarity. The problem was, the feeling was naturally very temporary and location-specific. I could get there on vacation, but it was not easily accessible living in the flatlands of Minnesota.

Midlife Crisis

As I approached my fortieth birthday and midlife, I found myself wrestling with much internal conflict. On one hand, I felt tremendously grateful for so many things. I absolutely loved being a mom to my three girls, I was finding success in my career, and mountain climbing had provided a much-needed sense of meaning and adventure. On the other hand, my relationship with my husband was failing terribly. Those red flags we had overlooked before we were married were now wreaking havoc on our relationship.

To be fair, I have to acknowledge I could not have been easy to live with. Living with someone who was in constant pursuit of something "more" had to be exhausting. What I saw as investing money in important life-changing ventures, he saw as wasting money. What I saw as searching for deeper meaning and purpose, he saw as being impossible to please. His reaction, at least from my perspective, was to aggressively, publicly, and stubbornly declare his unwillingness to make himself a victim of my irrational expectations. I perceived his behavior to be cruel, overbearing, and apathetic. I felt completely unloved and alone. Our mutual feelings of resentment and animosity created conflict in our home, and frequently led to uncontrolled emotion and ultimately, unpredictable chaos. Sound familiar? I refused to recreate that scenario for my children.

As I contemplated how to move forward, an interesting opportunity presented itself. My dad, uncle, brother, and I decided to go to Tanzania, Africa to climb Mount Kilimanjaro. At 19,340 feet, it is the tallest mountain in Africa and the tallest free-standing mountain in the world. Despite the fact that severe altitude sickness prevented me from reaching the summit of Kilimanjaro that time around, my experiences in Africa were truly life-changing. Six days on a mountain and the view looking down on the world below gives you a completely different perspective on life. I missed my girls terribly, but the thought of returning home to a marriage filled with animosity, emptiness, and negativity was too much to handle. I knew I had to be done.

Five months after my return from Africa my divorce was final. As far as I know, neither me nor my ex-husband spent another minute grieving the breakup of our marriage. My only regret was, and still is, the impact it had on my three little girls who were just thirteen and eleven (x2—twins!) at the time. Before our divorce was even final, their dad moved out of state and removed himself from their lives. It affected those three little girls.

As long as we are talking about causing your kids pain, let me tell you about my own contributions to that mess. While hiking Kilimanjaro I had become quick friends with our mountain guide. Despite the fact we came from completely different backgrounds and cultures, we had found a common bond. We both had a great love and passion for the mountains and were both searching for something more meaningful in life. During our many conversations he told me about his dream to expand his Kilimanjaro trekking business. I could not stop thinking about how I could make that happen. I could not stop thinking about the mountain, about Africa and my new friend. About the same time my divorce was finalized I had completed plans with my new African friend to start our own climbing and safari business. Oh, I forgot to mention: in addition to becoming business partners, my new friend and I decided to jump into a personal relationship as well. WTF! That also affected my three little girls.

My Destiny

For the next seven years, while working a full-time job, raising teenage girls alone and maintaining a household, I spent every spare moment of my life building a business with the man who I thought would love me forever. I cannot even put into words how exciting that time was for me! I felt like my life was oozing with purpose, meaning, and significance. It felt like my life had finally collided with my destiny and that all my wildest dreams were becoming reality. All my vacation time was spent traveling to Africa. During my visits I traveled across the Serengeti, spent time in remote tribal villages, and ventured off to romantic islands in the Indian Ocean. My biggest thrill was having the opportunity to summit Kilimanjaro on several different occasions, once sharing the experience with two of my daughters. I even learned a little Swahili! *Maisha mazuri*—life is good!

There were certainly risks involved in a lifestyle of mountain trekking and wandering across the world, especially when you are as accident- and incident-prone as me. My mishaps included tripping, falling, twisting ankles, puking my guts out, losing my toenails, breaking bones, and once being stretchered off a mountain. I have gotten lost and summited the wrong peak. I have had close encounters with bears and lions and have been in stand-off situations with a herd of elk and once with a cape buffalo. I have been stung by a jellyfish, swarmed by tsetse flies, contracted scabies, and after returning from one trip I was sent to the Center for Disease Control, since doctors could not figure out what I had. Despite all of that, I honestly loved every minute of my adventures.

Then one day, the man I thought would love me forever texted to tell me he was moving on. Just in case you were wondering if you read that right—yes, he *texted* me! He told me he was going back to his ex-wife and starting a new trekking business with a more prominent US investor. When I read that text, I literally could not breathe. I was devastated both emotionally and financially. I had invested my blood, sweet, tears and every penny I had into that business and I can honestly say I loved that man like I had never loved anyone before. In one day, it was all gone.

I used every ounce of energy I had to gracefully shut down the business and then promptly declared Chapter 13 bankruptcy. I no longer had any way to pay off the debt I had incurred investing in the business. Then another dose of reality hit me in the face: while I had been so busy trying to manage my chaotic adventurous life, I did not realize that my kids were struggling too. Remember that pit I was telling you about earlier? This brings us right to the edge of that.

Chapter 3

THE PIT

Things got very dark at the bottom of that pit. For those of you who can relate, you know that being lost in a pit that deep is a very dangerous place to be. I used every ounce of energy I had to get out of bed every morning, go to work, and to try and figure out how to help my girls. Things at home had escalated to the point where chaos had become a daily occurrence. I frequently had to call the police to help me get things under control. One of the lowest moments of my life was the Fourth of July when I watched the distant fireworks from the front seat of the ambulance that carried my emotionally broken daughter to the hospital. At one point I remember telling her that God loved her. I will never forget the look in her eyes and the sadness in her voice when she said, "What's the point, mom? Look where that got you." I had never felt like a bigger loser in my life. Not only had I landed in this pit, but I had taken my babies with me.

How could God allow this to happen? I trusted him, I had faith, I did what I was supposed to do, and he abandoned me. Worse yet, he had abandoned my children who did nothing to deserve this; they were just victims of their parents' foolishness and the cruelty of the world around them. I finally resorted to begging God for a sign that he cared about me or that he even knew that I existed. Nothing.

The only reason I did not completely give up at that point was because my girls needed me. I knew I needed to get them out of that pit and I had resigned to clawing my way out to do it. Every once in a while I would say a quick prayer in the unlikely event God even cared. I considered that the odds of him helping me were about the same as a Vegas crapshoot. Those were really difficult days! With the help and support of my amazing family and friends the girls and I got through that mess. Eventually, I was able to "get my poop back in a group" to function on the surface. But inside, things were not so good.

As I started to abandon faith in God, I realized that there was quite a void left in my life. Despite the fact that I spent the greater part of my life feeling lost and searching for purpose, meaning, and significance, at least I had held out hope that I would someday find it. That hope had now faded. I came to the realization that there likely was no purpose or meaning to life at all, and the reality was that I was completely insignificant. I tried to persuade myself that was OK, but I was not convinced.

Finally, I realized I had to make a decision. Either I believed in God or I didn't. There was no more back and forth, no more one day praying God would help me and the next questioning his existence. I needed to find the truth about God. Honestly, there was something very appealing about giving up the whole faith-in-God thing altogether. I considered that life could be a lot easier living with the freedom of not giving a crap about having to please an enigmatic God. The problem was, I couldn't do it. There was something still pulling me and telling me there was more.

I finally decided I would do a little research on the subject before completely giving up on faith and God. Maybe there was something I was missing? Maybe there was something I misunderstood? I mentioned earlier that I am an attorney, but I didn't mention that for the better part of my career I was a professional research attorney—and a pretty good one, I might add! If there was information out there that could help me sort through this mess, I certainly had the skills and resources to find it!

I started out by doing some preliminary internet recon (technical terminology for "Googling stuff") on the subject. I decided it would be helpful to set some baseline definitions and get an understanding of the different perspectives on the topic of faith and God. I found hundreds of resources and articles on the topic. From a purely religious and spiritual perspective, faith is generally defined as the choice to put one's complete confidence in God. *Webster's Dictionary* added another element which caught my attention: the "firm belief in something for which there is no proof."[4] Wait, what—no proof? I am an attorney, for heaven's sake! I don't believe in *anything* without proof! Or do I?

Curious, I had another question for Google: "Hey Google, is there any proof that God exists? That question opened a big old proverbial can of worms! I found some very strong opinions on both sides of that topic, but I was particularly interested in what critics had to say. Critics adamantly claimed there was no scientific evidence to support belief in any god(s). In fact, prominent and accomplished scientists said that belief in God was actually contrary to scientific discovery. They claimed there is substantial evidence supporting theories that the universe is the result of naturally occurring events; therefore, there is no logical reason to insert god(s) into the creation equation.

Yikes. I had certainly been aware of the differences between science and religion on issues such as creation and evolution. To be honest, I had always conveniently ignored the subject. As a Christian growing up, I of course learned the biblical story of creation found in the book of Genesis. God created the universe and the life within it in six days, and on the seventh day he rested. In school I learned about the Big Bang Theory and evolution—that the universe was the result of naturally occurring processes. Somehow, I kept the two divergent theories very separate in my mind. I guess I did not consider it relevant to my faith.

To the contrary, my research findings suggested it was all very relevant to faith in God. Many claim that science proves that the Genesis story is inaccurate, thereby proving that the Bible is inaccurate and that faith in God is naïve. I had never looked at it that way before. That got me thinking, "Hey Google, is the Bible accurate?"

Yikes again! It seems that there are many historians and other academic scholars who question the historical reliability of the Bible, and who particularly have issues with the Gospels that report the events of Jesus' life. Did you know that there are no original copies of the Bible, and that the earliest full-version text of the Bible is from the fourth century, three hundred years after Jesus allegedly lived? And that the Gospels are actually anonymous writings and there is debate about who actually wrote them? So, let me get this straight: We do not even know who wrote the Gospels that serve as the foundation for all Christian beliefs? Either I was not paying attention in religion class or that little fact was left out of the curriculum!

In addition to all of that, many also question the Christian religion based on philosophical grounds. They ask questions like, how can a good, loving and just God abandon his creation and allow such hardship, hatred, and injustice to prevail? Critics also recall the countless injustices that have been committed throughout the course of human history in the name of religion. Not to mention the daily hypocrisy of those who claim to be religious. When I began my little research project, I was emotionally questioning God. But after all this, I was now intellectually questioning the legitimacy of everything I once believed to be true.

At this point the only thing that was adding up for me was the fact that the dictionary definition of faith was spot-on, at least in my case. I had no proof to support what I believed. In fact, I could barely articulate what I believed, much less provide evidence to support it. As an attorney I am embarrassed to admit it, but what I had was more accurately defined as blind faith. All my life I essentially just believed what I was told to believe, without ever even knowing whether or not it was true.

It occurred to me that my faith—my blind faith, to be exact—was no different than Billy Backpacker's compass. My faith, it appears, was leading me to magnetic north. I was being pulled by misguided, inaccurate, and maybe even deceptive beliefs. And like the earth's magnetic north, those beliefs were constantly being changed and manipulated by worldly positions, circumstances, and forces. No wonder I was lost.

The question was, what to do about it? Part of me just didn't care anymore. I was confused, feeling quite duped and very tired. The problem was, I had taught my girls to have blind faith as well. I owed them more than that. If blind faith led to magnetic north, perhaps there was truth leading to true north? My goal was to find out. This is where my journey began.

PART II

DOES GOD EXIST?

PART II

DOES GOD EXIST?

Chapter 4

HOW DID THE UNIVERSE BEGIN?

I decided I needed to start at the very beginning. I needed to determine whether or not God even existed. Obviously, all other discussions about God were irrelevant if God didn't even exist. I began to read through countless theories presented by various philosophers, scientists, and theologians on the subject of God. I even read through some of the writings of Plato, Aristotle, Aquinas, Nietzsche, and many others whose names I could barely pronounce. To be honest, it was all so confusing that I wanted to give up before I even got started.

As I painfully pushed through the initial stages of my research, I stumbled on a question that seemed particularly relevant and related to the discussion of whether or not there is a God: *How did the universe begin?* It was a concrete place to start, so I decided to explore it. I quickly identified a huge problem, at least for me: *science!* Frankly, I hate science! I do not find it interesting and it did some major damage to my GPA in college! I took a few deep breaths to clear my mind. I realized I would just have to tackle this like every mountain I have ever climbed: one step at a time.

Lawyer Stuff

Before I ask you to walk through the results of my enormous research project with me, I feel I have to start with some lawyer stuff. I have a few caveats. If that term is not familiar to you, a caveat is simply a type of warning or stipulation meant to "CYA." Lawyers are really good at coming up with them to protect themselves from any kind of liability. I feel compelled to throw a few out before we get started.

Typically, people who do this type of research have a long list of letters behind their names, identifying them as experts on the topic. I will state for the record that I am not an expert or scholar in any area of science. The one (and perhaps only) expertise I would consider myself to possess is as a researcher. During my twenty-plus-year career as a research attorney I have researched literally thousands of legal issues and tackled projects I thought were impossible. I have learned to be patient and systematic as I sifted through volumes and volumes of material to uncover relevant pieces of information. I learned to assess the credibility of sources, to think creatively and analytically, and to organize information in a way that makes it manageable and understandable. Most importantly I have learned to push my way through confusion and ambiguity in order to gain the clarity needed to reach logical and informed conclusions and to find solutions to problems. I consider myself to be an expert researcher.

My research follows no particular methodology and likely cannot be considered academic nor scientific. All the information I am sharing with you has been gathered through the process of self-guided research, relying on information presented in hundreds of scholarly, theological, scientific, and philosophical articles and journals, and listening to countless hours of lectures, seminars, debates, and podcasts. I will admit that my bibliography is poorly lacking. I conducted my research over the course of many years, often jumping from resource to resource to try and make sense of what I was learning. I apologize if I do not provide the appropriate credit to my sources, but I do want to say how much I truly appreciate everything I have learned from so many along the way.

When addressing topics as complex and controversial as these, it is difficult to fully explain and cover all the relevant information on a topic. There are typically many different facets within each topic and each opinion. If I included all of it here, I would bore you to tears and kill a lot of trees. At the risk of oversimplifying some very complex topics, I will do my best to summarize the main arguments on both sides of issues and to review them as objectively, concisely, accurately, and straightforwardly as possible. Once I have presented the information, I will share my own personal conclusions with you. Please know that if you reach a different conclusion, I totally respect that. I would only ask that if you need more information in order to reach a decision for yourself, or if you question my facts or analysis, do some more internet recon on your own. Don't give up until you feel like you understand what you believe and why you believe it.

One last caveat: I have to warn you, these are some complex and sometimes mind-numbing topics. I will commit to making the journey as interesting as possible and hopefully worth your time. If you find the content puts you to sleep on occasion, that is a good thing! Let it soak in a little before you pick it up again. Rest in the fact that you are taking the time and effort needed to build a foundation for what you choose to believe and are no longer being guided by something you don't understand.

If you are with me, let's get this journey started!

Cosmology

Did you know there is an actual scientific field of study called cosmology? Cosmology is the study of the origins, development, and nature of the universe. There have been many different cosmological theories presented throughout history attempting to explain the origins and state of the universe. I think it will be helpful to have at least a basic understanding of these theories as we begin, so let me give you the quick and simplified lowdown on a few of them.

Way back in the fourth century BC, the Greek philosopher Aristotle believed that the earth was the stationary center of the universe and that the stars and planets revolved around it. Aristotle believed that the universe was finite (limited) in size, but infinite (unlimited) in time. That was generally the belief that was held for more than a thousand years. Then in the 1400s a Polish astronomer named Copernicus suggested that the sun was more likely the center of the universe. Copernicus theorized that the earth was in motion and rotated daily on an axis as it moved around the sun. By the 1600s, Galileo confirmed that Copernicus was right. Using his invention called the telescope, he could see that the earth and other planets did in fact revolve around the sun.

In 1687 Sir Isaac Newton outlined his theory of a steady state static (unchanging) universe. This theory suggested that the universe was neither expanding nor contracting and was therefore essentially without a beginning and always was. By the 1920s the theory changed yet again. A Belgian physics professor and Catholic priest by the name of George Lemaitre suggested that the universe was not static. Lemaitre said that the universe was in fact in a constant state of outward motion and was therefore expanding. He believed that if you were to trace that expansion backward in time it would necessarily have to originate from one particular point and therefore had a beginning. This theory was developed further by Edwin Hubble a few years later and eventually became known as the Big Bang theory.

Recently cosmologists have introduced a new theory for the existence of the universe called the multiverse theory. This theory actually revives some of the concepts of earlier cosmological thought—that the universe has no true beginning or end. The main idea is that our universe is not the only one that exists. Scientists theorize that there are an infinite number of universes existing in parallel with ours. The reason this theory considers the universe to have no beginning and no end is that scientists believe universes are continuously being formed in an infinite sequence of events.

Another viewpoint pertaining to the creation of the universe is the Genesis account of creation which is told in the Bible. Even though it is not considered a "scientific theory," it is another possible explanation for how the universe came into being. That story explains that God created the universe in six days. On the first day God created the heavens and the earth, and the story culminates with God creating man on the sixth day. Just for the record, there are some who believe the Genesis story of creation is a literal story, but there are many, including scientists, who believe that the Genesis account presents an illustrative story of creation and can complement scientific discovery to explain how the universe began.

It is important to remember that we categorize all of these explanations as theories for a reason. If you remember back to science class, a "theory" does not rise to the level of scientific law or proven fact. Instead, a theory is an acceptable explanation of a natural phenomenon based on careful examination of facts, but cannot itself be proven with 100% certainty. Theories are essentially the best guess that scientists can make based on information that is currently available to them. As technological advances continue to provide scientists with more information, there are likely to be new theories presented. That being said, the Big Bang theory is currently the prevailing theory for how the universe began. Let's take a look at the Big Bang theory in a little more detail, to see if there is anything that might shed some light on our ultimate question of whether or not there is a God who created this universe.

The Big Bang Theory

So, what is the Big Bang theory? Even though scientists describe it as a "big bang," it could probably be better described as the "big expansion" theory. As we saw earlier, the Big Bang theory is based on the observation that the universe is constantly expanding in an outward direction. Scientists theorize that the outward movement can be traced backward approximately 13.7 billion years ago to one single, very dense point, probably even smaller than the period at the end of this sentence. This concept is known as singularity, meaning that everything originated from that single miniscule micro-point which had to contain all the right ingredients to ultimately create the universe.

Scientists believe that the micro-point began to heat up, expanded quickly, and just kept growing and growing and growing. I picture it like one of those big bubbles you can blow when you are chewing a nice big juicy piece of bubble gum. The bubble starts out very small and then quickly expands. In the case of our universe, the bubble just kept expanding and within it emerged things like neutrons, protons, electrons, hydrogen, and many other important elements. Eventually, those elements started combining to make all the stuff we see in the universe today: stars, planets, galaxies, and ultimately life.

Scientists present as proof of this big expansion several different conditions they observe to be present in the far reaches of space. When looking into distant space through instruments like the Hubble Space Telescope, astronomers observe what appears to be a faint glow. They theorize that this glow is some type of thermal radiation, which they sometimes refer to as the cosmic microwave background. They believe that the existence of this radiation is likely the result of the original big bang event and that these waves of radiation are kind of like an echo that continues to emanate outward.

Another thing that scientists observe in far-off galaxies is something they refer to as redshifts. In physics, as objects move away from us the light waves are stretched into longer wavelengths which produce a reddish color. The existence of these redshifts would indicate that celestial objects are moving continuously away from us, again supporting the notion that a very powerful event set these objects into motion.[5]

Of course, there is much more to the scientific explanation behind the Big Bang theory. In fact, there is so much information on the topic it could keep a person reading for years. (Actually, it literally did keep me reading for years. I am lucky my head did not explode in a big bang-type scenario!) The main point and most important thing to note is that the Big Bang theory strongly supports the notion that the universe had a beginning at which point all time, space, and matter came into existence.

How Did It Happen?

If we assume that the Big Bang theory is accurate and our universe did in fact have some form of a beginning some 13.7 billion years ago, how did it actually begin? That is something scientists are unable to clearly explain. When scientists can't explain exactly how or why something happens the way it does, they rely on the laws (sometimes called theories) of nature to help them provide an explanation. Laws of nature were formulated based on years and years of repeated testing and consistent findings. These laws can describe with great consistency the patterns that nature will follow under certain circumstances.

The law of gravity is one example of a law of nature. We know that there is a force, which we call gravity, that pulls objects toward earth. We know that this force helps us keep our feet on the ground and keeps the moon orbiting the earth rather than flying off into space. We know that this force we call gravity exists based on consistent observations and experimentation that has led to almost 100% certainty that an object, when dropped, will fall to the ground (unless of course, it is a balloon filled with helium). We trust that this force exists despite the fact that no one has ever seen, touched, or heard gravity, and that scientists have no idea why it exists or how it actually works.

When scientists attempt to use the laws of science to help explain how and why the initial big bang took place, they are perplexed. The very existence of that initial singularity that supposedly caused the big bang is in complete contradiction with the laws of nature as we understand them today. This gets a little complicated, so hang in there with me. There are laws of nature that scientists call the laws of thermodynamics. Thermodynamics, very simply put, dictates the behavior of energy and explains how energy transfers from one place to another or from one form to another.

Let me try to give you an example of thermodynamics in action. As you know, water is comprised of two hydrogen atoms combined with one oxygen atom, good old H_2O. When water is exposed to temperatures below 32 degrees Fahrenheit it will freeze and become a solid in the form of ice. If you put an ice cube into a warm glass of lemonade on a hot summer day, the ice cube will melt and transfer the cool temperature (energy) to the warmer lemonade around it. We know that every time we put an ice cube in a warmer liquid that transfer process will occur. We know this because nature follows rules—in this case, rules that have been categorized as the laws of thermodynamics.

There are actually four laws of thermodynamics; we are going to focus on the first law of thermodynamics to help explain the initial singularity dilemma noted earlier. The first law of thermodynamics states that the total energy in an isolated system is constant; energy can be transferred or transformed from one form to another, but cannot be created or destroyed. A simpler way of summarizing the first law of thermodynamics is to say that "something cannot come from nothing."[6] When scientists attempt to explain how that initial singularity condition came to be, let's just say they run into some trouble with the first law of thermodynamics. Remember that we said the big bang expansion likely started as a very small, dense point. In order for that small point to expand and develop, there had to have been "something" in the form of matter or energy present. The million-dollar question is: Where did that "something" come from? The first law of thermodynamics says it could not have come from nothing. This is where I get really dizzy and want to quit, but let's push on.

Debate

As you might imagine, there are differing opinions as to how that initial singularity condition came to be. This debate seems to me to be highly relevant to the question we are hoping to answer: How did the universe begin? Let's check it out.

On one side of the debate are those who argue that the singularity condition, resulting in the big bang expansion and the development of the universe, can be explained in terms of naturally occurring events.

Essentially, they believe that there are only natural forces present in the universe and exclude anything considered to be "supernatural," meaning anything purportedly existing outside of our universe. This viewpoint or philosophy is often referred to as naturalism.

On the other side of the debate are those who believe that the existence of the universe can only be attributed to a creator, sometimes referred to as an intelligent designer. Many collectively refer to this side of the debate as creationism. It is important, however, to note that there are two distinctly different viewpoints within creationism. More about that in just a minute.

When you think about it, if the Big Bang theory is accurate and the universe in fact had an actual beginning, there are only two ways in which it could begin. The universe was either set into motion by unplanned, random natural events, or there was a force that set it all into motion. Now things are getting interesting!

Naturalism

Let's first take a look at the naturalist viewpoint. Let me start out by being completely upfront about something: despite reading through hundreds of articles and listening to numerous lectures and debates on this topic I am still not confident I have the ability to accurately summarize these arguments. The scientific jargon and mathematical equations presented to support their argument are, to put it mildly, way over my head! I had to push through a lot of information before I was able to gain even a basic understanding of this argument. Note that I am using the word "understanding" very loosely. In any event, here is my best shot at explaining the naturalist viewpoint on the beginning of the universe.

Remember the question we are trying to answer: If the Big Bang theory is correct and our universe began from a very tiny point of singularity, how did that singularity condition come to be when the laws of thermodynamics dictate that something cannot come from nothing?

The leading naturalist argument appears to be based on the theories of quantum physics, also referred to as quantum mechanics.

I know what you are thinking, because I thought it too: *Huh?* This is seriously complicated stuff, but stay with me just a minute longer and I think you'll get the idea. Quantum physics is the branch of physics concerned with how things operate at the subatomic (very, very, very tiny) level—so small, in fact, that the laws of thermodynamics do not apply. Remember we said earlier that the events culminating in the creation of the universe started out as a very small, dense point. The naturalism side of the argument says that you must look to the theories of quantum physics to explain how things may have operated in that very, very, very small, almost nonexistent, pre-bang condition.

Those proposing quantum physics arguments suggest that vacuum environments can help explain what may have happened. Vacuum environments are essentially the state of nothingness, presumably similar to pre-bang conditions. When studying vacuum environments scientists can observe unexplained, but measurable, energy fluctuations or disturbances. They call these fluctuations or disturbances, "lamb shifts." Very simply put, these lamb shift energy fluctuations suggest that there is "something" happening in that state of nothingness even though we cannot see it. Scientists hypothesize that these disturbances could be the result of particles spontaneously flashing in and out of existence. They categorize these theoretical particles as "virtual particles" because they have never actually observed them in a natural or even in experimental setting.

Scientists claim that events they refer to as "quantum tunneling" prove the existence of virtual particles. Quantum tunneling refers to the process where particles move through barriers, which according to the laws of nature should be impossible. They can actually observe electrons disappearing on one side of a barrier and reappearing on the other side, suggesting that virtual particles are potentially popping in and out of existence in the vacuum environment. As these particles become subject to gravity and start to crash into each other, they create a very unstable and chaotic environment. As best I can tell, scientists believe this type of environment could have created the singularity condition that expanded into the universe we know today.[7]

I think it is important to reiterate that more recent theories of cosmology, like multiverse theories, suggest that our universe is only one of many. These theories tend to downplay any notion that the universe had a definite "beginning." Since the multiverse theory argues that the universe is just part of an infinite sequence of fluctuation type events, there is no need to explain an actual beginning.[8]

I don't know about you, but I have a quantum-induced headache! That is about the extent to which I am able to reasonably summarize the naturalism theories to explain the existence of the universe. Honestly, I tried for months to wrap my head around these concepts and I know I have only scratched the surface of understanding them. At the risk of sounding scientifically illiterate and being far too overly simplistic, I believe the main point of the naturalism argument is that the existence of the universe, whether it had a beginning or whether it has existed forever, can be explained by purely natural events that happened as a result of random and unplanned chance.

Creationism and Intelligent Design

Now let's look at the arguments presented by creationists. I mentioned earlier that there are two main subgroups within the creationist camp. Before we go any further, I would like to talk more about these two very divergent viewpoints.

The first group is frequently referred to as "young earth creationists." Earlier, I mentioned the biblical story in Genesis. There are some Christians, including some scientists, who argue that the Genesis story is a literal account of creation and hold firm to the notion that God created the world in six, twenty-four-hour periods. They are referred to as "young earthers" because they contend that the universe is very young as opposed to billions of years old. Based on a very literal reading of Genesis they believe the earth to be in the range of only six thousand to twelve thousand years old. To support their argument, the young earthers argue that things like carbon aging could have occurred at differing rates over time, skewing the results of carbon dating and the age of bones and other fossils.[9]

For the record, I did take considerable time and effort to try and understand their arguments. To be honest, I have had a very difficult time wrapping my mind around their arguments and could find very little evidence to support their claim that the universe is less than twelve thousand years old. I have personally chosen not to include their arguments here as part of my research study, but that does not mean they are not worth considering. If you are interested to learn more about the young earth creationist arguments and assess them for yourself, I would encourage you to do some further internet recon on your own.

The second subgroup frequently categorized as holding a creationist viewpoint is referred to as intelligent design. It is important to note that those arguing intelligent design theories hold very different views than those of the young earth creationists. Intelligent designers, in many instances, are cosmologist and scientists who on many levels agree with naturalists concerning how the universe likely developed. The primary difference is that intelligent designers believe the evidence supports the fact that some kind of intelligent designer was at work in that process rather than it being the result of random and unplanned events, as naturalists suggest. I should note that not all intelligent designers will even refer to this designer as "God." For the most part, those supporting intelligent design theories agree that the identity of the intelligent designer falls outside the scope of scientific discussions.

To support their theory, the intelligent design side of the debate relies heavily on evidence that the universe is highly complex and finely tuned. They essentially argue that it would be impossible for this level of complexity and fine-tuning to happen as a result of random, unplanned chance.

I would like to explore the intelligent design arguments in more detail—but before we do, I think it is important to take some time to understand the level of complexity within the universe around us and what the concept of fine-tuning actually entails.

Chapter 5

HIGHLY COMPLEX AND FINELY TUNED UNIVERSE

I think it is impossible to deny that there is some extremely complex and amazing stuff in our universe. This complexity is often referred to as the "fine-tuning" of the universe. Let's take a look at just a few of the countless examples of the complexity found within our universe. Check this out.

The Razor's Edge

The razor's edge represents the precise conditions, called constants, that must be present in order for life and the universe to continue to exist. Here are just a few:

- The existence of matter (tangible stuff) relies on a precise nuclear force to hold atoms together. If that force were to vary even by .1%, protons would no longer be able to bond to neutrons. If that were to happen, the universe could only contain hydrogen gas and all other matter would cease to exist.

- The ratio of the electromagnetic force to gravity is precisely balanced. If it would deviate even slightly, the electromagnetic force would overtake the gravitational force making life within the universe impossible.

- The rate at which the universe expands must remain at a precise constant of one part in 10^{55}. If the rate of expansion was even slightly faster, the formation of stars and planets would be impossible; and if it was even slightly slower, the universe would risk collapse.[10]

The Earth

The earth's size and corresponding gravitational pull holds a thin layer of exactly the right mixture of gases to sustain plant, animal, and human life. This layer of gases, known as the atmosphere, extends about fifty miles above the earth's surface. Earth is the only known planet equipped with this spiffy atmosphere. Without it, life on earth would be impossible and our planet would probably have conditions similar to that of Mercury. The earth is exactly the right distance from the sun, allowing the entire surface of the earth to be properly warmed and cooled every day. (However, I question that proper-warming thing during February in Minnesota.) If the earth were any closer to the sun we would burn up, and if we were any further away we would all freeze. The earth rotates around the sun at a constant speed of 67,000 mph. In fact, the earth moves around the sun with such consistency that we can establish with precision the measurement of "time" in days, months, and years. The moon, rotating around the earth, is the perfect size and distance from the earth to create ocean tides. The earth's hydrologic cycle takes the water that evaporates from the earth's surface into the atmosphere and distributes it in the form of precipitation. That water then sustains and nourishes vegetation, animals, and people across the globe.[11]

The Living Cell and DNA

DNA, also known as deoxyribonucleic acid, is the basis for life on earth and is contained in almost all living cells. (Little-known fact: DNA is not found in red blood cells!) DNA is an incredibly complex molecule and takes the form of a double helix, resembling a twisted ladder. The ladder stores sequenced codes, based on what is essentially a four-letter code or language. That coded information provides specific instructions to the cell. It tells the cell what life form the organism will take—for example, whether the life form will be a plant, insect, animal, or human being. The DNA code will provide each cell instructions on how to function for example as a brain cell, heart cell, or muscle cell. It will also dictate what traits the cell should express. In the case of a human being DNA carries instructions for eye and hair color, whether a person will be short or tall and countless other characteristics.

Last but not least, DNA carries and conveys instructions for reproduction, which will pass information on to the next generation. Because the DNA genome or code is unique to each individual person, there are no two people exactly alike—not even identical twins. To give you an idea of how much information is stored in DNA, consider this: if you were to stretch out the DNA found in just one human cell, it would be about two meters long. Scientists estimate that the human body at any given time contains about 37 trillion cells, which means that the DNA information found in one human body would stretch around our solar system . . . twice.[12]

The Human Brain

As you sit here reading, your brain is doing some amazing things. It is processing information by taking in letters and words that you see, translating them into meaningful information, and then storing that information for future use. Your brain is assessing the temperature around you to let you know if your body is cold or hot. It is keeping track of your bodily functions, controlling your breathing pattern and heartbeat, and even keeping track of whether you are hungry or not. It is processing your emotions and thoughts, which determine whether you are feeling tired, bored, happy, or sad. These are just a few of the things your brain is doing at this very moment.

The human brain consists of about a billion neurons and makes more than 100 trillion connections. As advanced as computer technology has become, there is no computer as efficient as the human brain.[13]

The question is, how did all this complexity and fine-tuning happen? We saw earlier that naturalists believe the universe is the result of unplanned, random, and naturally occurring events. We will see in a moment that they also believe that the complexity and fine-tuning of the universe is the result of unplanned and unguided events. Those supporting the intelligent design theory, however, argue that the level of complexity present in the universe is far more likely the result of intelligent causation rather than that of pure chance. Let's look at some of the arguments for intelligent design.

Intelligent Design Theories

There are several arguments that intelligent designers use to support their position. On a very foundational level, they first have had to defend their theory as legitimately scientific. The reason for this is that many opposed to the intelligent design theory maintain that the detection of "intelligence" falls outside the scope of science altogether. In response to that challenge, intelligent designers argue that the detection of intelligence is used as a matter of general practice by many in scientifically related fields. For example, they note that forensic scientists look for evidence of intelligent cause or intervention to establish whether a death was the result of natural causes or whether there is evidence that a deliberate mind contributed to a murder. Archaeologists look for signs of intelligent design to help them identify ancient tools and artifacts. Arson investigators sift through charred remains, looking for evidence of chemical accelerants indicating the presence of intelligent intervention. Organizations like SETI (Search for Extraterrestrial Intelligence) continuously search outer space for evidence of intelligence in the form of meaningful messages or intelligent activity. While naturalists commonly categorize the detection of intelligence as unscientific, intelligent design supporters contend it fits squarely within its definition.[14]

One of the leading arguments offered to support the intelligent design theory is based on the statistical improbability that our highly complex, finely tuned, life-supporting universe was created by random chance. There have been many mathematical calculations and statistical scenarios presented to support this argument, but I will highlight one in particular that caught my attention.

Sir Roger Penrose is an English mathematical physicist and philosopher (let's just call him a genius). In the 1960s he collaborated with the world-famous cosmologist Stephen Hawking to develop the concept of the initial big bang singularity we looked at earlier. Penrose calculated the probability that the initial singularity condition could have contained all the right stuff to develop into the finely tuned universe we experience today as 1 in $10^{10^{123}}$. To give you some perspective on how inconceivable these odds are, consider that a 1 followed by twelve zeros makes a trillion. The odds that our universe was the result of unplanned, random, and naturally occurring events are immeasurably smaller than 1 in a trillion (1,000,000,000,000) chance.[15] Intelligent design proponents often use probability calculations such as these to argue it is much more likely our universe was the result of intelligent causation rather than random chance.

Another leading argument offered to support intelligent design focuses squarely on the existence of DNA. Those that support the intelligent design theory argue that the very existence of DNA unquestionably infers that an intelligent force has been at work in the universe. As we saw earlier, DNA contains "information" essentially equivalent to a written language or computer code and provides specific instruction to each living cell. Intelligent designers argue that it is impossible for "information" containing this level of complexity to be the result of random, unplanned chance. To support this argument, they refer to the research findings of mathematician, philosopher, and theologian William Dembski. Dr. Dembski argues that when information exhibits "specified complexity," there is fundamentally sufficient evidence to support a design inference. He defines specified complexity as information that is both complex (in the sense it is highly improbable to have occurred) and specified (which means it is arranged in a sequenced pattern which produces specific results). Intelligent design supporters argue that scientific methodologies, including observation, experimental testing, and repeated verification, definitively prove that information which is specific and complex has intelligent causation.[16]

Another intelligent design argument worth mentioning relates to a time in the earth's developmental history called the Cambrian period. Approximately 540-plus-million years ago, during a time now referred to as the Cambrian Explosion, the fossil record reflects a sudden influx of new life forms. Intelligent designers argue that many of the major animal phyla (or life family categories) we find existing today appeared for the first time during the Cambrian period.[17] They note that the sudden appearance of new life forms at this time could only be the result of new information introduced into the system, as there would not have been enough time for natural processes such as mutations and natural selection to occur. Additionally, they note the lack of what are known as "transitional fossils," which would evidence gradual changes between specie groups over time.[18] Intelligent design supporters argue that the only thing that would explain such an increase in new life forms is an influx of new information, which would naturally infer an intelligent contributor.

While many assume that intelligent design supporters would oppose theories of evolution, it is important to note that this is not the case. Most supporting intelligent design theories agree that there is ample evidence showing evolutionary progression within specific specie groups over time. They refer to this process as microevolution. This differs from the naturalist concept of macroevolution which theorizes that life has evolved from one species to a completely different and unique species. Intelligent designers argue that if this were the case there would again be more evidence of transitional fossil.

There are, of course, many other arguments presented by the intelligent design group to support their theory.[19] I have tried to capture and summarize what seem to be the leading and most prominent arguments. I encourage you to do further research on the topic if you are interested in learning more about the intelligent design theory. In summary, I believe it is fair to say intelligent design supporters contend that the fine-tuning of the universe and the specified complexity of DNA can be best explained and scientifically evidenced to be the result of intelligent causation rather than unplanned, undirected natural processes.

Naturalist Theories

Earlier we explored naturalist theories regarding the way in which the universe began as a result of naturally occurring, unplanned, random chance events. Let's now explore the theories they present to explain the fine tuning of the universe and the existence and development of life within it.

First, let's look at how naturalists account for the beginnings of life on earth. In the 1920s scientists first proposed a concept they referred to as chemical evolution (sometimes also called abiogenesis). They suggest that life was the result of a step-by-step chemical evolutionary process which served to transform nonliving material into the first life form. Naturalists theorize that the very first stages of chemical evolution took place roughly 4.6 billion years ago in conditions they refer to as the "primordial soup." The surface of the earth was primarily covered in water and simple elements such as hydrogen, ammonia, and methane were abundant in the earth's atmosphere. The theory suggests that during this first stage, these simple elements began to bond together to form amino acids, likely aided by energy produced by lightning.

Naturalists suggest that the second stage in the process occurred when the amino acid molecules began to bond together to create larger molecules such as proteins. By stage three, they contend those protein molecules combined to create something scientists refer to as "photobionts." Photobionts are aggregate molecules that while technically considered nonliving material, for the first time presented the very rudimentary characteristics of life. While there is much yet undefined about what actually occurred during these stages, naturalists claim they have been able to roughly simulate these natural processes in a laboratory setting.

It is theorized that the last phase of the chemical evolutionary process occurred when photobionts developed the capacity to reproduce. An organism's ability to reproduce and pass on its DNA to the next generation is one of the essential characteristics defining "life." Those supporting naturalist theories acknowledge they cannot currently provide a complete explanation for how nonliving material ultimately transformed into living material, nor can they explain the existence of the complex DNA code within it. While they cannot currently provide a complete explanation for the existence of life on Earth, they are confident that continued research will provide them with the information needed for a better and more complete understanding of the process.[20]

Naturalists use theories of chemical evolution to explain the beginning of life on Earth. In order to explain how life developed over time, they turn to theories of "biological evolution." We have all likely heard this process referred to as the "theory of evolution," which was first proposed by Charles Darwin in the 1850s. Darwin theorized that life originated from a single life form. (As a note of interest, Darwin never considered the question of how life on earth initially came to be, but was only interested in how it changed over time.) As that life form reproduced, there were small changes that took place from one generation to the next. After millions of years, these small incremental changes resulted in diverse and prolific life forms. Darwin used a tree, often referred to as the "tree of life," as a metaphor to describe the relationships between the different life forms and how they could be traced back to common ancestors.

After time, these life forms became highly adapted to their environments, making them very efficient and effective and better suited to survive. Darwin theorized that this process of adaptation, was the result of what he called "natural selection." The theory of natural selection suggests that life forms possessing genetic traits and characteristics more advantageous to survival will thrive and pass those traits on to the next generation, while those that have less favorable genetic traits will be eliminated. Naturalists today continue to rely on the theory of natural selection to provide an explanation for the complexity of life on earth. They acknowledge that the process of natural selection can give an impression of design, as intelligent designers suggest, but in reality the complexity of life can be attributed to these naturally occurring processes of natural selection.[21]

To support the theory of evolution, naturalists offer as evidence the world's massive collection of fossils, which they refer to as the fossil record. Fossils are, of course, ancient life forms that were preserved in a petrified state or the impression of their remains left behind. Naturalists contend that the fossil record serves as evidence that life became more prolific and complex over time. We saw earlier that intelligent design supporters often challenge evolutionists, claiming the fossil record lacks sufficient transitional fossils to prove the transformation from one life form to another. Naturalists respond to these criticisms by presenting evidence of what they deem to be many transitional fossils. They also point out that while many transitional fossils exist, it is unrealistic to expect a complete fossil record as environmental conditions and natural circumstances did not always allow for the preservation of every living organism.[22]

To further support their theory, naturalists contend that DNA provides conclusive evidence for evolution. In the 1950s when scientists James Watson and Francis Crick discovered that DNA was passed on from one generation to the next, they finally had evidence for what they had been assuming all along. They could prove that traits were in fact passed down from generation to generation just as Darwin suggested. Naturalists contend that life likely originated from a single life source, and that as it reproduced over time it mutated and changed. Natural selection weeded out weaker life forms, and those containing traits more suitable to life in the surrounding environment survived. Naturalists contend that by using an organism's DNA, they can reconstruct its evolutionary history and show relationships between life groups. In short, they argue they can now use DNA as evidence to prove that there is a common link between all life forms, which in turn serves as evidence of evolution.[23]

To explain the overall fine-tuning of the universe, naturalists often turn to the multiverse theory. As noted earlier, there are many very specific conditions required to sustain the existence of the universe and the life found within it. Earlier we learned that multiverse theories suggest our universe is just one of possibly an infinite number of universes that exist. Given the fact that there are literally unlimited different possible universe scenarios, they contend that ours happens to be one of perhaps many capable of creating and supporting life. Naturalists acknowledge this is a new and developing explanation for the fine-tuning of our universe and that there is much more to learn, but argue it presents a reasonable explanation for the finely tuned conditions found in our universe.[24]

Once again, naturalism presents much more to support their arguments than I have been able to include here. For our purposes, I think it is important to note that naturalists argue that purely natural processes can explain the fine-tuning of the universe and the existence and development of life within it. Naturalists do not claim to currently possess the knowledge and understanding to completely explain every detail of how the universe and life came to be, but they believe that time and continued scientific discovery will eventually fill in those gaps of knowledge.[25]

This brings up one last quick point. Naturalists often refer to intelligent design arguments as being a "God of the gaps" argument. This term refers to the tendency people had throughout history to attribute unexplainable phenomenon to be the work of a god/s. The many Greek gods of ancient history are examples of this. Zeus was the god of the sky who hurled lightning bolts, and Poseidon was the god of the sea who caused storms and earthquakes. Of course, over time science provided natural explanations for things like lightning and earthquakes, so the gods lost their power so to speak. Naturalists categorize intelligent design as just another "God of the gaps" argument and believe that the existence of the universe and life will someday be completely explained by science; we just have not gotten there yet.[26]

For more information, find references to some great debates and discussions on the topics of the existence of God, the universe and life.[27]

Chapter 6

DECISION TIME

I don't know about you, but I have had about as much science as I can possibly absorb. I am officially scientifically exhausted! I must admit, I am surprised by the amount of information I was able to get through and to understand, at least on some level. You should be very proud of yourself for hanging in there as well. This information can be very overwhelming and a bit mind-numbing. Good for both of us pushing through it and taking the time to educate ourselves on these very difficult topics!

Before sharing my final decision with you, I would like to start out with a caveat. I know I have mentioned this several times already, but I think it is very important to note again that there is much more to both the naturalist and intelligent design theories than I have been able to include here. I did my best to include what appeared to me to be the leading arguments and evidence presented by each side of this case. I apologize to you scientific types out there if you feel I have unfairly oversimplified the highly complex scientific data and information involved in research of this type. I tried my best to present it in a way that is accurate but not impossibly overcomplicated. If you feel I have overlooked other relevant arguments or misrepresented any of the information I presented, I would love to sit down to talk!

With that, I think we are equipped with the information needed to make an educated decision for ourselves. I will share my own personal analysis and decision on these issues with you, but I encourage and expect that you will take the time to weigh the evidence for yourself and make your own decision. As I have said before, the most important thing is that you take the time to understand what you believe and why you believe it, rather than simply relying only on what someone else has told you to believe.

Decision-Making Process

I am inclined to approach my decision-making process the same way a jury is instructed to reach a verdict in a court case. While the scenario and decision before us are admittedly different than one presented in a courtroom, I believe the process can help guide us to a well-reasoned final decision on the issue. In a court case the jury has three primary responsibilities. Let's quickly review them, to make sure we have a good understanding of what is involved in the process.

The first step is to review the evidence proposed by each side of the case. Once the jury has heard the evidence, they must determine what evidence they believe to be accurate and reliable in order to establish the facts of the case. In other words, they piece together the evidence to reconstruct a picture of what likely happened. Once they establish the facts, they will use them to reach a final decision.

Because the evidence can rarely give jurors a complete picture of what happened, they have to arrive at a decision by drawing "inferences." An inference is the process of connecting pieces of evidence to a final conclusion. If you are like me and relate better to visuals, try this: Visualize one of those wooden suspension bridges that hikers use to make their way across a river out in the wilderness. If that bridge is missing several of its wooden planks, leaving huge open gaps, people are less likely to rely on it to take them across. On the other hand, if the bridge looks sturdy and there are no large gaps between the planks, people will feel confident using it to get to the other side. An inference is essentially a bridge. If there are huge gaps in evidence, logic, and reason, people are not going to rely on it to get them to the conclusion on the other side.

Before we dive in to make a decision on the very serious and important issue before us, I thought we could take a minute to talk through a simple and less scientific example of how the decision-making process flows and the importance of evidence, facts, and inference.

I have a little dog named Daisy Duke. She is about six pounds soaking wet and cuter than a button, but she has a reputation for being very naughty! The other day I took Daisy Duke with me to do some errands. I was hungry so I stopped to get a hamburger, which I left in the Jeep with Daisy while I ran into the bank. When I came back, the hamburger bag had been ripped open, the hamburger was missing, and Daisy Duke had ketchup all over her pathetic little face. To top it off, when I went to scold her, she burped!

Let's say that Daisy Duke is now on trial and we are the jury. The issue before us is whether Daisy Duke is guilty of ham-burglary. Daisy Duke's defense attorney claims she is innocent. He argues it is possible that a pigeon squeezed through the open window, ripped open the bag, grabbed the hamburger, and framed Daisy Duke by rubbing it in her little face before taking off with it. Since no one actually saw what happened, our task is to determine whether the evidence (ripped bag, missing hamburger, ketchup, and belch) more reasonably and logically infers that Daisy Duke ate the hamburger or a pigeon took off with it. I don't think we would have to deliberate long. Based on our observations and experiences, we know it is much more logical to infer that Daisy Duke ate the hamburger versus that whole pigeon theory. Once we, as the jury, establish the fact that Daisy Duke ate the hamburger, we can use it to reach a verdict. I am guessing we would find Daisy Duke guilty of ham-burglary in the first degree!

Calling to Order the Case
of Naturalism vs. Intelligent Design

We set out to answer the question, does God exist? In an effort to answer that question we looked at two related issues: 1) How did the universe begin? and 2) Who or what is responsible for the complexity and fine-tuning of the universe and the life existing within it? We learned that there are two main theories providing possible answers to these questions. The first is the theory of naturalism, which suggests that the universe and the existence and development of life within it can be explained by purely naturally occurring processes and the result of random, unplanned, and unguided chance. The second is the theory of intelligent design, which suggests that the universe and the existence and development of life within it has an intelligent cause. Ultimately, one of them is right. The question is, which of these conclusions is best supported by the evidence offered?

Evidence and Facts

As the jury in this case, we have a very important decision before us. We have already completed the first step in the process, which is to hear the evidence. We may not have uncovered every piece of relevant evidence out there but I think it is safe to say we gave it our best effort and conducted our due diligence.

The next step in the process is to use the evidence to establish the facts. Because the evidence in our case is so complex, this could prove to be an extremely challenging and daunting task. To keep things as manageable and objective as possible, I would like to propose a list of facts that I not only believe the evidence supports but that both naturalists and intelligent design supporters would likely agree on. Of course, each side might have some slightly different nuances, but I think for the most part this gives us a fair and balanced set of facts to move forward with.

- The universe likely began with a big bang type scenario somewhere in the ballpark of 13-plus-billion years ago;
- The universe operates according to consistent laws of nature that have guided its development and govern how it operates;
- Approximately 3.5 billion years ago, the first signs of life emerged on planet Earth;
- Fossil records reflect that over time, life forms changed and became increasingly more prolific and complex;
- All living organisms are made up of cells which contain DNA, which in turn contain the instructional code needed for an organism's development, survival, and reproduction;
- The very existence of the universe and life within it is dependent on extremely precise and finely tuned, improbable conditions, if those conditions vary even slightly, our universe and life within it will cease to exist.

The next step in the process is to use these facts to reach a decision on the issue before us. To do that, we need to determine if the facts establish a stronger inference (bridge) to naturalist theories or intelligent design theories. Here is my own verdict.

My Decision

I have to begin by acknowledging that I was not able to answer the question I initially set out to research. I cannot honestly say that my research findings, on their own, led me to a definitive conclusion about whether or not there is a God. I cannot even claim to have answered questions of how the universe began, or what is responsible for the fine-tuning of the universe we experience today. I have only been able to reach a definitive conclusion on one very specific issue. I find the evidence reasonably and logically infers and supports the conclusion that DNA, carrying the instructions for life, has intelligent causation. Let me explain the reasons for my findings and what I think this means in terms of my journey to find true north.

It seems to me that application of the scientific method alone makes it logical to infer that DNA is the work of an intelligent mind. According to Merriam-Webster, the scientific method is defined as "principles and procedures for the systematic pursuit of knowledge involving the recognition and formulation of a problem, the collection of data through observation and experiment, and the formulation and testing of hypothesis."[28] Throughout the course of human history, observation and experiment consistently reveal that information with any level of specified complexity has intelligent causation. If that is the case, how is it logical to consider DNA, which literally carries the coded instructions for life, as the one and only exception to this rule?

I searched for anything to refute this conclusion, including looking for examples of information that has been determined to be the result of unplanned and undirected natural processes. While naturalists frequently claim that the process of natural selection can give the false appearance of design, I could find nothing that would explain the creation or existence of information as a result of natural process. In fact, I was surprised to find that even extremely low, simplistic levels of information have provided sufficient evidence to infer intelligent causation. For example, consider archeologists, who by simply identifying multiple fracture lines running in the same direction can distinguish an ancient handmade stone tool from a plain old everyday rock.[29]

Let me give you a personal example that I think will help further illustrate this point. When hiking in the mountains at lower elevations, it is fairly easy to find and follow the trail as it is generally well worn into the ground by the hundreds of trekkers who have gone before you. When you get above tree line, over about 10,000 feet, it is easy to lose track of the path, since there are often large stretches of nothing but rock where the trail is not evident. If you are lucky you can rely on cairns to help guide you. Cairns are simple rock piles that have been built by hikers before you to help mark the direction to the summit. Despite the fact that you are standing in a sea of rock, a pattern of small rock piles presents enough information to confidently infer that someone has been there before you and was kind enough to provide you with directions.

It is concerning to me that patterned fracture lines and rock cairns can provide enough information to infer intelligent input, yet naturalism adamantly claims that DNA is the result of unplanned, unguided naturally occurring processes. It is particularly concerning when by all accounts, DNA can be considered the gold standard of information, containing extraordinary elements of specified complexity. Remember, specified complexity means the information is not only highly complex and unlikely to occur by chance, but also contains and conveys information in the form of instructions which carries out specified results. Even Bill Gates, cofounder of Microsoft, admitted, "DNA is like a computer program but far, far more advanced than any software ever created." DNA is actually considered equivalent in complexity, if not more advanced, than computer programing code. That is intense!

Here is another real-life example to give you more context around the concept of specified complexity. In Estes Park, Colorado, where I frequently go to hike, there is a rock formation on the edge of town that resembles the shape of two owls perched next to each other. The formation is fittingly referred to as Twin Owls. The formation certainly reflects a level of complexity, as it is a very improbable formation. While the formation has a level of complexity and improbability, I don't think anyone questions whether or not it was caused by naturally occurring processes.

Now, let's say we are hiking and see ahead of us four intricately detailed faces carved into the side of a mountain. Not only is the formation extraordinarily detailed, making it extremely complex and highly unlikely to have occurred by chance, but it presents a highly informative pattern, as it represents four admired former United States presidents. How many people do you think would argue that Mount Rushmore was the result of random, unplanned, naturally occurring processes?

I don't think there is any question that if naturalists were to discover this level of specified complexity in any other scenario, they would conclude it to be the work of an intelligent mind. Why then do they conclude that DNA—containing perhaps the most sophisticated levels of specified complexity ever known to man—is the result of unplanned, unguided random chance? I believe the answer lies in their adherence to the philosophy of material naturalism. Material naturalism is the notion that only natural laws and forces operate in our universe.[30] Anything outside those parameters would be considered "supernatural," which they contend falls outside the purview of science. If they acknowledged that DNA has intelligent causation, then intelligent cause would naturally have to exist outside the boundaries of our natural universe; therefore, the possibility of intelligent design is "unscientific." Do you see where this is going?

My question is, why does science and particularly material naturalism take such a strong stance on this issue? I can give you my opinion. Earlier it was noted that in the past people, including many religiously motivated people and organizations, attributed unexplained phenomena to the acts of god/s. Scientists able to provide a scientific, natural explanation for the events were often criticized, and sometimes even imprisoned and violently punished, for their views. Luckily scientists, despite the risks, challenged this limited thinking and encouraged broader, more open-minded logical thinking. Over time as scientific discoveries advanced, we as a society began to embrace scientific explanation and eventually considered acts of god/s to be superstitious and ignorant explanations for naturally occurring events—the "God of the gaps" mentality.

In light of history, my question is this: Is it possible we have now swung too far to the other end of the spectrum and adopted a "science of the gap" mentality? Is it now only acceptable to consider "scientific" explanations for things like DNA, despite the fact that science cannot provide an answer or at least a scientifically acceptable answer? I believe the answer is increasingly becoming yes. At the risk of sounding like a dreaded lawyer and getting all political on the subject, I am going to jump on a big old soapbox for a moment.

In the United States today, many of our public-school science teachers are required to teach their students that DNA is the result of random, unplanned, and unguided natural events. They are not even allowed to suggest or discuss the possibility that DNA has intelligent causation, and here is why: In 1987, the United States Supreme Court, in the case of Edwards vs. Aguillard (107 S.Ct. 2573) ruled that teaching biblical creationism in public science classes violated the Constitution's establishment clause requiring the separation of church and state. In 2005, the Unites States District Court of Pennsylvania, in the case of Kitzmiller vs. Dover Area School District (400 F. Supp 2d 707; MD Pa 2005) ruled that the theory of intelligent design is essentially equivalent to the teachings of biblical creationism. Hence, the court in that case ruled that teaching the theory of intelligent design in public schools in the State of Pennsylvania is unconstitutional. By the way, many other school districts across the country have adopted this stance as well. While the Kitzmiller issue has not yet been addressed by the United States Supreme Court, when that happens (and it will), their ruling will be binding in all public schools in the United States.

Based on my research and everything I have learned, I find the Kitzmiller decision quite concerning. First of all, it clearly seems erroneous to say that intelligent design and biblical creationism are the same or even similar theories. They are two very different and distinct points of view. While biblical creationists rely on the Bible as their main source of information to explain the creation of the universe, intelligent design relies only on scientific based findings to explain causation. Throughout my research, it has been my experience that scientists supporting intelligent design and scientists supporting naturalism hold similar views in terms of the mechanics of creation and the development of the universe. The main difference is that one side argues creation has intelligent origin, while the other argues it was all the result of unplanned chance.

The second reason I take issue with the Kitzmiller case is that in my opinion it limits the importance and value of critical-thinking skills. Like scientific thinking, critical thinking includes elements of observation, understanding, analysis, evaluation, inference, and logic.[31] Perhaps the main difference is that critical thinking is not limited by the tenets of material naturalism and valid in any discipline. I completely recognize that the study of science has greatly benefitted our society, technologically transforming the way we live and contributing to the overall well-being of the human race. However, I think instituting a "science of the gaps" mentality has the potential to be as harmful and dangerous as a "God of the gaps" mentality.

Perhaps we as critical thinkers should take a cue from scientists of the past, who demanded broader, more open-minded thinking with the hope of gaining a more complete understanding of our universe. Don't get me wrong; I am in no way suggesting that science teachers should suddenly proclaim the existence of god/s, or even mention the word "god," for that matter. I do, however, think we ought to teach our young people to consider and weigh reasonable evidence for themselves. To restrict that information and tell them what to believe sounds a little bit like a magnetic-north kind of scenario to me! With that, I will as gracefully as possible step down off my soapbox!

If I were given the opportunity, I would have a few questions for those supporting naturalism, since I have not been able to find answers through research efforts. If considering the existence of an intelligent force outside the boundaries of our universe is deemed to be unscientific because it cannot be scientifically tested, is considering the possibility of multiverses outside the boundaries of our universe also unscientific? How can we scientifically justify the conclusion that DNA, the most highly complex and specified information ever known to exist, has natural origins when scientific testing has consistently concluded that even the smallest amounts of information have intelligent causation?

In my opinion, the fact that naturalists deem DNA to be the result of random chance has more to do with denying what intelligent design would imply rather than with scientific integrity. If naturalists acknowledged the possibility that DNA has intelligent origin, they would essentially be acknowledging the existence of an intelligent force outside the boundaries of our universe. As we can probably guess, the next likely step is calling that intelligent force God.

I will be the first to admit that the existence of God makes absolutely no logical sense whatsoever. If you think about it, the belief in god/s has been the impetus for many atrocities throughout the course of human history. I certainly relate to feelings of disdain for the hypocrisy of so-called "religious" people who condemn and destroy others physically and emotionally in the name of "God." I relate to the resentment of religious institutions that have forced their moralistic and even scientific beliefs down people's throats, often leading to injustice and oppression. I relate to the confusion felt about any intelligent designer or god who could allow such chaos and tragedy to exist within the confines of their creation. Honestly, I think it would make a lot more sense if we were to conclude that the universe is controlled by nothing more than neutral and impartial natural forces. The problem, at least for me, is that I have proven to myself that this, too, is not logical.

So where does this leave me on my journey to determine if there is a God? Honestly, at this point in my journey, I am not sure. I can tell you that this journey has been intensely challenging. I set out to determine whether God actually exists, and the truth is, I did not find the answer to that question through science and logic.

I did, however, uncover information that left me wanting and needing to know more. While I cannot speak with the expertise of a scientist, I can speak as someone who has conducted their due diligence on the subject. Based on my research findings, I can say with certainty that I believe DNA, the instructional code for life, provides evidence and a strong inference for intelligent causation. If you have weighed the evidence for yourself and reached a different conclusion, I completely respect that. As I have said before, the most important thing is that you have taken the time to better understand what you believe and why you believe it.

My journey, however, is not complete. I now find myself asking: Who is this intelligent designer? If you find yourself asking the same question, I invite you to continue with me on my journey.

PART III

WHO IS THE INTELLIGENT DESIGNER?

PART III

WHO IS THE
INTELLIGENT DESIGNER?

Chapter 7

RELIGION

I spent a lot of time trying to better understand how our universe operates, in the hope it would give me some insight into whether or not there is a God. While I did not actually find the answer to that exact question, I did prove to myself that there is evidence of some form of intelligent force at work in our universe. The question of "God" still remains open. While science may have helped us up to this point, it cannot bring us any further. The next question is: Where can I find credible and reliable evidence that can shed some light on the identity and nature of this intelligent force?

I once again began my research by doing some internet recon on the subject. It quickly became apparent that throughout the course of human history this "intelligent" force has largely been identified as "God." (I should mention there are some who suggest that the intelligent designer could be aliens from another galaxy, but I am going to set that one aside for the moment.) So, is there any empirical, verifiable evidence as to who this intelligent force or God actually is?

The only source I was able to find offering information about the character and nature of God is in the context of "religion." I must admit, my immediate reaction to this news was not very positive. In my mind, religious belief is much more about tradition, ritual, and emotion than anything that can be supported with evidence, reason, and logic. I looked for other ways to approach the study of God, but all trails led back to religion, so I guess that is where I will start.

Webster's Dictionary defines religion as "a personal set or institutionalized system of religious attitudes, beliefs and practices."[32] There are about 4,200 different religions practiced around the world today, and they all have different opinions about God. Obviously, it is not practical to study 4,200 different perspectives about God, so I went in search of another approach.

As I continued to poke around a little more, I discovered that 75% of the world's population belongs to one of five major religious groups: Hinduism, Buddhism, Judaism, Christianity, and Islam. Many of the remaining 4,195 religions are in some way derivatives of these core religious beliefs or are very small, localized, tribal-based religions.[33] Since these five religious groups represent the far majority of the world's population and have all obviously had a great deal of influence and impact on our world, I think it makes sense to begin our study here. While I will not be able to cover every aspect of each of these religions, I will do my best to summarize their origins, core beliefs, authoritative texts, and religious practices.

Hinduism

Origins: Hinduism is believed to be one of the world's oldest religions, possibly dating back as far as 5500 BCE. It is believed to have originated in India, where it continues to be an important and dominant belief system today. While Hinduism is technically considered a "religion," it can probably more accurately be described as a way of life, as it has had great influence on the social systems and customs across India. There is a great deal of complexity and diversity within Hinduism as beliefs and practices evolved over the course of many centuries and within localized subcultures. Despite that diversity, there is a core set of beliefs common to most Hindus.

Core beliefs: Hinduism can actually be considered both or either a pantheistic religion (meaning that God is essentially one with the universe) or a polytheistic religion (meaning that they believe in many gods). Hindus typically believe in a universal force or essence they refer to as Brahman. This force is formless, limitless, eternal, and encompasses everything seen and unseen. They believe that the entire creation emerged from, rests in, and will dissolve into this one source of all being.

Under the blanket of Brahman are three main Hindu deities who each have different areas of authority and power. They are known as Vishnu, who is considered the preserver God; Brahma, who is considered the creator God; and Siva who is considered the destroyer God.

There are thousands of other Hindu gods with lesser power, who take many different forms. An example of one of the better-known and beloved Hindu gods is Ganesh. This god is depicted as having a human body with an elephant head. Ganesh is a very important Hindu god as it represents the soul. Hindus believe that the soul is eternal and part of the universal force of Brahman which makes all life sacred. They believe that souls are reincarnated and pass through a succession of lives. Their status in their next life is dependent on the way they lived their previous life. This concept is known to the Hindus as *karma,* which is essentially the constant link between actions and consequences. The ultimate goal of a Hindu is to break the cycle of life and death which they call *moksha.* In *moksha,* the soul is liberated from the body, unites with the universal force, and achieves oneness with nature.

Authoritative texts: Because Hinduism is an ancient practice, and predates the existence of written languages, the first Hindu traditions were likely handed down from generation to generation via oral transmission. As the written language developed, traditions were documented in Hindu texts known as the Vedas. The Vedas collect and document poems, rituals, and the teachings of various sages (wise teachers) over time, and document the Hindu understanding of the universe and what they believe to be absolute truth. The Vedas are rich in metaphors and primarily written in the ancient Sanskrit language, which is very hard to translate into modern languages. It is believed that the Vedas collection likely started somewhere around 2000 BCE, making it the oldest known religious text in the world.

Other Hindu sacred texts include the Upanishads, which is a series of writings that document some of the central beliefs and philosophies of Hinduism. The writings making up the Upanishads were likely collected sometime between 800 and 300 BCE. Perhaps one of the best-known Hindu scriptures is known as the Bhagavad-Gita, which means "Song of the Lord." The Bhagavad-Gita is considered to be the world's longest poem. It was likely written sometime around 300 BCE and primarily tells the story of Krishna, who is one of their better-known deities.

Religious practices. Hindu worship is primarily practiced on a personal level rather than as a community. Hindus worship either in temples or in their own homes, where they set up shrines to conduct daily worship. Worship typically consists of repeating mantras and offering sacrifices, which they believe brings them into closer relationship with the gods. The ritual of sacrifice is believed to appease the gods in order to avoid punishment for their wrongdoings and typically consists of food, fruit, water, flowers, or incense.[34]

Buddhism

Origins. Buddhism began in about 500 BCE as an offshoot of Hinduism. The founder of Buddhism was a man named Siddhartha Gautama, who eventually became known as the Buddha. Siddhartha was born in Nepal in about 563 BCE to a wealthy Hindu family. At about the age of twenty-nine, Siddhartha realized that his great wealth and status were not providing him happiness and fulfillment. Siddhartha ultimately renounced his family title, left his wealth behind, and became a poor monk in search of a better way of life and human happiness.

After six years of study, Siddhartha found what he called "enlightenment." It was then that he became known as the Buddha. Enlightenment, he believed, was the key to human happiness and contentment.

Buddha traveled extensively, teaching others about the way to enlightenment, until his death at about the age of eighty. Buddhism eventually spread throughout India, Nepal, Tibet, China, Japan, and the Asia-Pacific region. While not many in Western cultures practice Buddhism as a religion, its teachings and philosophies have gained much popularity as a method of meditation and in the context of ethics.

Core beliefs: Buddhism is officially considered a religion, but many would say it is really a philosophy or way of life. Buddhism is considered neither a monotheistic, pantheistic, nor polytheistic religion since there is generally no concept of god/s recognized in their belief system. Buddhists do not deny the existence of god/s but acknowledge it is impossible to define who that god is. Buddha himself never focused on a divine creator or any god/s in his teachings.

There are many different schools of Buddhist thought, which makes it difficult to identify one clear definition or understanding of their beliefs. The main teachings of the Buddha, however, are typically at the core of their beliefs. Buddha taught that in order to reach the state of enlightenment, people should understand and acknowledge the Four Noble Truths. Ultimately the goal of Buddhism was to attain the state of *nirvana* at death. Nirvana is not believed to be an actual place, but a transcendent consciousness where there is perfect peace and all desires and suffering have been extinguished. The goal of nirvana can technically be attained by anyone, but believed to be realistic for very few. One who finally achieves nirvana becomes known as *a* Buddha. "*The* Buddha" will always be in reference to the original Buddha, Siddhartha Gautama.

Short of achieving enlightenment, the goal for most Buddhists is to generate enough good karma in order to gain a higher existence in their next reincarnation. As we saw earlier, karma is the belief that a person's actions result in consequence, good deeds being rewarded and bad deeds punished. While Hindus believe that karma is determined by the gods, Buddhists believe that karma operates as a result of natural law. They believe that karma will impact the form of life following reincarnation, which could be in the form of human, animal, or plant life.

Authoritative texts: Buddha himself never wrote down any of his teachings. Earliest Buddhist teachings were passed down orally through the use of repetition and poetic and mnemonic verses. The first Buddhist texts started to appear around the first century BCE. There are many different versions of Buddhist texts, but one of the most important is called the Sutras. The Sutras are considered to be the conversations and sermons of Buddha and some of his close disciples. There are twelve Sutras that are organized by the topic and the style in which they were delivered. The Sutras are considered to be the words of Buddha.

Religious practices: Today many Buddhists live according to the teaching of Buddha, but they do not actually worship Buddha, or really worship anything for that matter. It is clear that Buddha never claimed to be any form of god and rejected attempts by his followers to worship him. Buddhists do attend temples where they frequently go to meditate and clear their minds. They typically chant and meditate sitting on the floor, often facing a statue or image of Buddha. The Buddha statutes are present only as a reminder of his teachings and as an expression of gratitude for his contributions to the world.[35]

Judaism

Origins: Judaism is another ancient religion, with its origins dating back to about 2000 BCE. A man named Abraham is considered to be the father of the Jewish faith. Abraham was born in approximately 2166 BCE in the area of what today is known as Iraq. Polytheism (the worship of many gods) was widely practiced during this time in history. When Abraham was approximately seventy-five, God was believed to have spoken directly to him. This god identified himself as the one and only true God to be worshipped. God made a covenant (deal) with Abraham. God promised that if Abraham would worship him, he would in return make Abraham the leader of a great nation. God promised Abraham that this great nation would be formed from his descendants and that the land would be blessed.

While Abraham, along with his wife Sarah, trusted God enough to leave their homeland in search of God's Promised Land, they did not understand how God would provide them with the descendants he promised them. He and Sarah had reached old age and had not had any children. Abraham and Sarah decided that in order to have descendants as God promised they needed to take matters into their own hands. They arranged for Abraham to have a relationship with one of Sarah's maids named Hagar. Hagar eventually gave birth to a son named Ishmael. (This will become relevant later, when we discuss the religion of Islam.) God's intended plan, however, was that the new nation would begin with a baby born to Abraham and Sarah. In spite of their age and disobedience, God gave Abraham and Sarah a son who they named Isaac. Isaac's lineage became the nation of people who lived in the land God promised to Abraham, which became known as Israel.

Core beliefs: Judaism is the world's oldest monotheistic religion, which means belief in only one God. Most central to the Jewish belief is that the God who revealed himself to Abraham some four thousand years ago is the one and only true God and is perfect, just, merciful, holy and father and king over all creation. They believe that God is omnipotent (which means that God can do anything), omnipresent (which means that God is everywhere), and omniscient (which means that God knows all things).

Many important Jewish leaders came through the lineage of Abraham. Some of these special people in Jewish history are referred to as prophets. Prophets are people who the Jews believed conveyed important messages from God. Perhaps one of the most important and best-known Jewish prophets was Moses. It is believed that sometime around 1300 BCE Moses led the Jewish people, who had become slaves in Egypt, back to the land God had promised Abraham. This event became known as the Exodus, part of which Jews continue to commemorate today during the Passover festival. Jews believe that on the journey back to the Promised Land God gave Moses the Ten Commandments, to serve as moral guidance to the Jewish people.

Other important prophets in Jewish history foretold that God would someday send the nation of Israel a messiah. The word "messiah" means "anointed one," which referred to a king. The Jews believed that this king would be a great charismatic political leader who would make Israel the most powerful nation on Earth. Over the centuries several people have claimed to be the Jewish messiah. Perhaps the best-known claim was that made by Jesus of Nazareth. (This will become relevant when we discuss the religion of Christianity.) Many Jews rejected his claim and to this day await the coming of the promised messiah.

Authoritative texts: Jews typically refer to their Holy Scriptures as the Tanakh or the Hebrew Bible. It is a collection of ancient writings by different Jewish authors that document the origins, history, and messages of the Jewish faith. The first five books of the Hebrew Bible are known as the Torah and are believed to have been written by Moses. It includes narratives about the origins of the Jewish people, documents the law, and records covenants that God made with the Jewish people.

The Talmud is another Jewish scripture. The Talmud is a collection of oral laws that were passed down from generation to generation and were eventually compiled in written form. More conservative Jews believe that the Talmud is authoritative Jewish law and needed as a supplement to truly understand the Torah. There are two parts of the Talmud. The first part of the Talmud is called the Mishnah and is a collection of Jewish oral traditions that were written down sometime during the second century CE. The second part of the Talmud is called the Gemera and contains rabbinical analysis and commentary harmonizing the Torah and Mishnah teachings.

Religious practices: Prior to the year 70 CE, the temple in Jerusalem was the main headquarters for Jewish worship and community. The sacred temple was destroyed by the Romans in 70 CE to retaliate against Jewish rebellion to Roman rule. When the temple was destroyed, so too were important lineage records and sacred artifacts. Those identifying as Jewish today could be referencing either their religious beliefs or cultural ethnicity. Those of the Jewish faith generally consider actions and behavior much more important than beliefs. Traditionally Jews believed that to live a good life and to draw closer to God they needed to follow the divine commandments, which they called *Mitzvot*. The Mitzvot is made up of 613 commandments which generally instruct people on how to live their lives.

Those practicing the Jewish religion today typically belong to one of the branches of Judaism referred to as Orthodox, Conservative, or Reconstructionist. These various branches of Judaism differ in their approaches to worship, adherence to tradition, and the way in which they interpret the Jewish scripture. Jews typically worship at synagogues where they meet for prayer and religious worship. Prayers are recited out loud as a community which serve to worship God and as a way to continue to build relationship with him.[36]

Christianity

Origins: Christianity is a religion dating back to around 33 BCE, when many of the Jewish faith believed that the long-awaited Jewish messiah revealed himself on Earth as the person of Jesus of Nazareth. Jesus was believed to have been born sometime between 6 and 4 BCE in the city of Bethlehem. When Jesus was about thirty years of age, he began to teach publicly and claimed to be not only the Jewish messiah but the Son of God. He was eventually killed because of what many considered to be his outrageous and blasphemous claims. Jesus' teachings became the foundation for what later became a more organized religion which was eventually referred to as Christianity.

Core beliefs: Christianity is considered a monotheistic religion, but many find their definition of "one God" confusing. While Christianity is an extension of belief in the Jewish God who revealed himself to Abraham, they believe that God manifests himself in three different persons. Christians believe that there is one God (in essence) formed by God the Father, who is the Creator of all that is; God the Son, who is Jesus sent to Earth; and God the Holy Spirit who lives within each believer, providing them help to live like Jesus.

Today there are many different branches of the Christian faith called denominations. While beliefs vary slightly within each denominational group there are core common beliefs that unite them. Christians believe that Jesus was conceived by a woman named Mary through the power of the Holy Spirit, so was therefore both God and man. During his ministry Jesus was believed to have performed many miracles and taught a message of peace and love, encouraging people to love their enemies and to love God with all their hearts, minds, and souls. Many believe that Jesus' primary message and purpose for coming to Earth was to save people from their sins so they are able to live with God in heaven for eternity after their death on Earth. Perhaps Jesus' most prominent message was that he came to reclaim his creation from evil and to establish the kingdom of God in the hearts of believers.

After about three years of public ministry, at about the age of thirty-three, Jesus was convicted by Jewish religious leaders of blasphemy, for claiming to be God. Jewish leaders also convinced Roman officials, who politically controlled the region of Israel at the time, that Jesus was guilty of treason. They argued that by claiming to be the king of the Jews he threatened the authority of Rome, which was a crime punishable by death. The Romans violently beat and then killed Jesus by means of crucifixion. Jesus' followers claimed he rose from the dead after three days and that they saw him alive again after his death. Christians believe that Jesus will return to Earth again someday, at which point he will take back physical control of the earth and eliminate all influences of evil.

Authoritative texts: The Bible is the primary sacred text of the Christian faith. The Christian Bible is made up of two main parts, the Old Testament (which is essentially the Jewish Bible) and the New Testament. The New Testament includes the biographies of Jesus which they call the Gospels, and other writings by followers of Jesus which talk about the growth of the early Christian church. Christians typically believe that the Bible is the Word of God, which was written by people but inspired by God.

Religious practices: Christian denominational groups include Anglican/ Episcopal, Assembly of God, Baptist, Lutheran, Methodist, Presbyterian, and Roman Catholic. They mainly differ in terms of ritual practices, but have some minor theological differences as well. Worship services are typically held on Sundays each week and range from formal to informal services which include prayer and Bible study.[37]

Islam

Origins: Islam is a religion dating back to about 610 CE when a man named Muhammad began to receive revelations from Allah (Arabic for God) through the angel Gabriel. Allah is believed to be the same God to have approached the Jewish prophet Abraham many centuries earlier. Muhammad began receiving revelations when he retreated to remote caves to meditate and continued to receive revelations from the angel over the course of the next twenty-three years. Muhammad is considered by Muslims to be the greatest and final prophet in the line of Jewish prophets starting with Abraham but extending through his son Ishmael, who we learned earlier was the son of Hagar.

Around the year 621 CE Muhammed was taken by the angel Gabriel on a journey to Jerusalem in Israel on a winged animal. This night journey is referred to by Muslims as the Mi'raj. The angel brought Muhammed to the site of the Jewish temple which had been completely destroyed in 70 CE by the Romans. From there Muhammad ascended through seven layers of heaven where he encountered Abraham, Moses, and other prophets. It was here that Muhammad is believed to have received instructions on how Muslims were to pray. Today the Dome of the Rock shrine commemorates that site in the city of Jerusalem.

Core beliefs: Islam is another of the world's monotheistic religions. Muslims believe God's chosen people descended through Abraham's firstborn son Ishmael, not Isaac as the Jews and Christians believe. Of central importance to Muslim belief is that Allah is the all-powerful, all-knowing, merciful, and compassionate creator of all that is and the one and only true God. "Islam" is the Arabic word for *surrender*. Muslims believe that the purpose of human life is to surrender to Allah as his servant and to show complete devotion to him through worship and by following his commands. They carry this out in their daily lives by practicing the *five pillars* of Islamic faith: 1) reciting the *shahada*, which is their profession of faith; 2) *salat*, which are prayers that must be conducted five times per day facing the direction of Mecca (Islam's most holy city); 3) *zakat*, which is a form of tithing; 4) fasting, particularly during Ramadan; and 5) *hajj*, which is to participate in a pilgrimage to Mecca at least once during a person's lifetime.

Authoritative texts: Muhammad recited the revelations he received from the angel back to his companions (followers). His companions memorized the verses which were later recorded in the Quran. Muslims consider the Quran to be the divine word of Allah. Muslims believe that the Quran is a continuation of the revelations Allah revealed to previous Jewish prophets including Moses who was given the Torah, David who was given the Psalms, and Jesus who was given the gospel. They believe that God's messages recorded in the Jewish and Christian Bibles were corrupted and changed over time and that Allah sent the words of the Quran as a correction to those messages. Muslims believe the Quran is incapable of alteration and that it is meant to be Allah's final message to people on Earth.

While the Quran is the primary authority which instructs Muslims how to live in relationship to Allah and each other, they have other sacred texts as well. The Sunnah is another source of primary authority which outlines traditions and practices that provide more practical detail and instruction regarding the Quran's basic commands. As an example, the Quran dictates that prayer to Allah is essential, but the Sunnah specifies the obligation to pray five times a day. The Sunnah was collected by the companions of Muhammad who listened to his messages, and observed his behavior and the way in which he lived his life. The companions of the Prophet then handed these instructions down orally from generation to generation until they were eventually compiled in written form.

The Hadith is another set of Islamic scriptures that Muslims use as instructions for living. This collection includes the sayings and practices of Muhammad which serve as guidance to Muslims today on how to live a good and acceptable life surrendering to Allah. There are several different collections of Hadith, totaling about 75,000 different stories. Some of these collections are accepted by some Muslims as authentic and rejected as unauthentic by others.

Religious practices: Today there are basically two different branches of Islamic belief: Sunni and Shia. While there are variations in the way each branch practices their faith, they share most of the fundamental Islamic beliefs. The Islamic holy scriptures provide Muslims direction on how to live every aspect of their lives including guidance on worship, personal relationships, business dealings, and societal issues and responsibilities. Daily prayers typically include recitation of verses from the Quran and are always conducted in the direction of the *Qibla,* which means that it is done facing the direction of Mecca, Saudi Arabia. Prayers can be conducted individually or as a community, which is usually conducted at a mosque. A mosque is a Muslim house of worship, but also commonly used for community and social gatherings.[38]

So, What Does This Mean?

Trust me when I say we have covered just the tip of the iceberg as it pertains to religion. If you are curious to learn more, I would highly encourage you to do some further study on this very interesting topic. Per usual, I have a couple caveats before we move on.

First, it is important to note that believers within each religious group can fall on a spectrum from devoted followers to those who simply identify with a particular religion for family or social reasons. It is important we do not inadvertently lump all religious believers into the same category.

The other thing I think is important to note is that simply studying these religions cannot provide a full and complete picture of what they are all about. Much can be gained by actually experiencing the different ceremonies, traditions, emotions, and conviction of believers. Those experiences bring to life and humanize what are otherwise just concepts. Some of my richest educational moments have been the opportunities I have had to observe and even participate in religious ceremonies very different than my own.

Aside from being very educational and interesting, though, what does this all mean? Up to this point I have proven to myself that there is some form of intelligent force that has intervened in the development of the universe at least on some level. Historically, that intelligent force has been defined as some form of a god/s. Religious institutions seem to provide the only definitions of god/s, but each holds a very different view about the nature and identity of who that god/s is. How do we now determine which of them is right—or better yet, if *any* of them are right? My question is this: Is there anything by way of objective, unbiased, verifiable evidence to determine if any of these religious claims are accurate?

During my initial internet recon on the subject it became quickly apparent that most religious followers do not spend much time focused on providing evidence to support their beliefs. If you ask most believers what evidence they have to support their beliefs, they might respond with something like this. "I believe Christianity to be true because the Bible is the infallible Word of God, so therefore it serves as evidence that Christianity is true." At least that is the circular reasoning I often used in the past to defend my beliefs about Christianity. I guess if I am really honest, I would have to add as evidence the fact my mom also told me it was true! In my defense, and in the defense of many, regardless of their religious beliefs, evidence is typically not a topic addressed as part of religious education. Where then does one look for evidence to verify religious belief?

I struggled to find ways to verifiably test religious claims about God. It seems that neither Hinduism nor Buddhism made any attempt at all to defend their beliefs with evidence. I guess that makes sense, since neither really makes any religious claims about God. In addition, many of the claims made by Judaism, Christianity, and Islam are very subjective, as they are based on personal revelation which cannot be objectively verified. It also seemed to me that the evidence presented by all three religions was surprisingly similar, essentially in presenting the same broad-stroke arguments, at least on the surface. All three claim their scriptures were inspired by God, which they contend is evidence that their beliefs are true and accurate. They also all argue that the fact that their traditions and scriptures have been preserved for hundreds and thousands of years should serve as evidence of their historical accuracy. While it is not my intent to criticize any of these arguments, it seems to me that none of them offered any sort of objectively verifiable evidence.

As I continued to dig deeper, I finally stumbled on something that caught my attention. Being raised a Christian, I was of course always aware of the claim that Jesus of Nazareth was God who came to Earth as a man. What I had not considered, however, was the opportunity the claim presented. Christians are essentially claiming that God inserted himself into the course of human history, and they have ancient writings that supposedly record the events. Even more interesting is the fact that both Jews and Muslims acknowledge that Jesus was a person in history, and their religious texts talk about the guy too.

Of course, they all have differing opinions about who Jesus was. Christians claim Jesus was the Son of God, and their Gospels report that he was executed on a Roman cross and later rose from the dead. Jews believe that Jesus was a guy in first-century Israel claiming to be the Jewish messiah. The Jewish Talmud refers to him as a type of sorcerer. Muslims believe Jesus was a great prophet of God. The Quran claims that someone looking like Jesus died on the cross in his place and that Jesus himself never actually died. The Quran makes the additional claim that it is the only true and accurate version of history which was revealed by God to Muhammad and that the Jewish and Christian scriptures contain inaccurate and corrupted messages.

It occurred to me that historically examining these accounts could on some level present us with the opportunity to objectively test these religious claims. Some quick internet recon revealed that the study of history, like science, has well-established guidelines and criteria for assessing the reliability and accuracy of historical claims. They refer to these as "historical methodologies." Now things are getting interesting! Anyone interested in exploring some history with me?

Chapter 8

HISTORICAL METHODOLOGIES

History is the academic discipline focused on reconstructing the past. Our understanding of what happened in the past, and particularly the ancient past, is limited to what we find preserved in writings or handed down via oral traditions. In some circumstances, archaeology can also provide us with an understanding of what happened in history. Because it is difficult to know if accounts about the past are accurate and it is important to distinguish fact from myth, legend, or exaggeration, historians have developed a set of guidelines and criteria they refer to as historical methodologies. Historical methodologies can help historians determine if information is more or less likely to be historically accurate and reliable. While historical methodologies can never definitively prove what happened in the past, they can help to assess the historicity, or historical reliability, of the information.

Since we are looking to assess the historicity of claims made about Jesus of Nazareth, I think it makes the most sense to begin by applying these historical guidelines and criteria to the Christian New Testament Gospel accounts. The Gospels presumably document the events taking place during the life of Jesus. Before we do that, I would like to begin by telling you what I was taught about the Gospels growing up. I think it serves as a good example of how not everything you are taught to believe is necessarily accurate. Let me tell you what I mean.

Growing up in the Christian faith I had been taught that the Bible, including the Gospels, is the authoritative and perfect word of God. I had been taught that Matthew, Mark, Luke, and John wrote the four Gospels about Jesus. I personally understood that these four men were disciples, or at least acquittances of Jesus, making them eyewitnesses to the events they wrote about. As I learned more about the history of the Gospels, I realized that what I had been taught was not necessarily correct. It turns out that the earliest Gospel texts never actually identified the authors, which technically makes them anonymous writings. It also turns out that even if these four men actually did write the Gospels, likely only two of them personally knew Jesus or witnessed the events taking place during his lifetime. So much for the eyewitness testimony credibility I had previously placed a great deal of stock in.

I also learned that the Gospel accounts contain notable inconsistencies and sometimes even contradict each other. That definitely put a dent in the idea that they were somehow perfect or inerrant as I had learned. In addition to that, I found out that the Gospel texts we have today are actually the product of copies of copies of copies and various different translations over the centuries. I am not sure why, but I was surprised to learn that we do not possess any of the original Gospels and that the earliest full-text version in existence today is from the fourth century. That certainly draws into question the reliability of the Gospel texts.

I would really like to know how it is possible that I attended Catholic schools from kindergarten through twelfth grade, regularly went to church services for many years, and had never heard of these concerns before now. It quickly became very clear that I had a lot to learn about the historicity of the Bible, the accounts of Jesus, and my own religious beliefs.

As I am sure you can imagine, there is a great deal of debate about the historical reliability of the Gospels. Historians and scholars are extremely divided on the issue. Some apply the historical methods to the Gospel and conclude that they can in no way be considered historically reliable. Others apply the same tests and conclude they can be considered reliable. Before we actually start digging into our historical test, let me tell how I plan to attack this research.

I will once again start by warning you about the nature of this content. I found it to be almost as complicated and sometimes as mind-numbing as the scientific topics we looked at earlier. Absorbing it all can be challenging, but I encourage you to hang in there with me and digest it in small doses if needed. This information offers some very good insight into the credibility of the writings concerning Jesus of Nazareth and whether the Christian claims are reliable.

There are three main categories of tests historians use to assess the historical reliability of ancient writings. Keep in mind, these historical guidelines not only apply to religious writings but to any writing of a historical nature. I will detail the individual guideline considerations within each category and briefly summarize arguments presented by both sides of the debate. I will also include my own personal opinion on how the Gospels measure up to each test.

Since there are several tests, I have decided to institute my own informal personal point system in order to track my overall assessment on the writing's historicity. If I find the writing meets the criteria, I will award it a point. I completely acknowledge this is a very informal and nonacademic way of reaching a decision, but I think it will help me work through the process and put me in a better position to ultimately weigh the evidence for myself.

One other quick note: in addition to the four Gospel writings—which, remember, are the first four books of the New Testament and purport to record the events taking place during the ministry of Jesus—I will also be including some of the letters written by the apostle Paul. The letters of Paul were written during the early years of the Christian church, offering spiritual guidance to different Christian communities. While Paul never lived or worked directly with Jesus during his ministry, his writings provide insight into the teachings of Jesus and the claims he made. For that reason, we will include several of his writings in our analysis as well. With that, let's roll!

Internal Tests

The first set of guidelines we will look at are collectively referred to as the "internal tests," or sometimes as "source criticism." These guidelines specifically assess the historical reliability of the information source, its trustworthiness, and its relevance. The internal tests ask things like when the information was recorded, who wrote it, and how the information was presented. Here are a few of the internal tests historians apply to assess the reliability of information about the past.

Internal Test #1:
Timing and the Importance of Early Attestation

The purpose of this criterion is to establish the date when the original documents were written and compare that to the date of the actual events. The earlier the details of an event were recorded, the stronger the indicator for historical reliability. The concern is that as time passes memories fade and things like exaggeration, legend, and false claims can creep into the narratives.

As I mentioned earlier, we do not currently possess any of the original writings. During the first century, authors typically wrote on a material called papyrus. Papyrus is a paper-like substance made from reeds that grew in the rivers. The originals and many of the earliest copies likely deteriorated long ago. On occasion historians and archeologists will locate copies, or parts of copies, they call manuscript copies. They use those available manuscript copies to conduct their tests.

There is quite a bit of uncertainty as historians and scholars attempt to assess the timing of the Gospel writings and letters of Paul. The manuscript copies never indicate the dates when the events actually occurred, nor do they provide dates for the writings. For that reason, scholars and historians have to rely on cues within the writing to help them determine dates. Because there is no way to pinpoint the exact dates, historians generally propose a range of possible dates.

I created a little cheat sheet for myself in an attempt to help assess the time gaps between events and the writings. The dates below represent the date ranges which appear to be accepted by the majority of both Christian and non-Christian historians and scholars. I have also included the estimated time gap between the actual events and the dates of the writings.

Writing/ Approximate date of original/ Time gap following death of Jesus (assuming 30 CE)
Gospel of Mark/ 66–70 CE/ Max 40 years
Gospel of Matthew/ 80–90 CE/ Max 60 years
Gospel of Luke/ 85–90 CE/ Max 60 years
Gospel of John/ 95–110 CE/ Max 80 years
Letters of Paul/ 42–63 CE/ Max 33 years

Debate: The primary question when applying the "timing test" is whether or not the date of the original writing is close enough in time to the events to indicate historical reliability. Remember, the more time that passes between the time of the events and the writings, the less likely they are to be reliable.

As you might guess, scholars are divided on this issue. Christian scholars tend to argue that the timing test weighs in favor of the documents' reliability. They argue that the New Testament documents were written relatively close to the time of the events when compared to other historical writings of antiquity. For example, the writings about the life of Caesar were written about a thousand years after he died. Writings about the life of Aristotle were written about 1,100 years following his death. In comparison, the twenty-five-to-eighty-year time gap for the Christian writings seems relatively small.

Non-Christian scholars and historians, on the other hand, suggest that these time gaps diminish the credibility of the Christian sources. Many question why the authors of the Gospels would have waited such a long time to record the events if these events were indeed as remarkable as they claim. They also contend that the Gospels appear to present content that was influenced by exaggeration and legend, due to the supernatural nature of their claims. Exaggeration and legend tend to make their way into accounts about the events as times passes.[39]

My personal assessment of reliability: When assessing the timing test, I think it is important to reiterate that we cannot view the timing of these writings through a twenty-first-century lens. As I sit here today writing on my computer with spellcheck and the internet which gives me access to the world's resources at my fingertips, yes, the time gaps seem unreasonably long. If we look at the time gaps through a first-century lens, however, the time frames sound reasonable. I imagine it was difficult to secure writing supplies in those days and that these authors presumably had a lot going on. They likely faced limitations and challenges we cannot even imagine today. While the Christian documents do appear to be early in comparison to non-Christian writings, I am not fully convinced by these arguments, so I am inclined to stay conservative on this issue and give it a half point for historicity.

Natalie's Points: +.5

Internal Test #2: Eyewitness Testimony

The next historical guideline pertains to whether or not the Gospel accounts contain eyewitness testimony or if the accounts are based on what we would call, in a court of law, hearsay. In court, eyewitness testimony carries much more weight than the testimony of someone who learned about the events secondhand. The same holds true for this historical test. If the evidence suggests that the accounts were compiled based on eyewitness testimony, they are considered more likely to be historically reliable than those that were not.

Debate: The question is, can historians provide enough reliable evidence to determine whether or not the Gospel authors were eyewitnesses to the events?

It is undisputed that the Gospel texts themselves do not identify the authors. Non-Christian scholars argue that since the documents do not reference the identity of the authors, nor do they contain any references to their sources of information, they cannot be considered the product of eyewitness testimony.

Christian scholars argue that early church leaders in the late first and early second century formally identified the authors of the Gospels. They contend that it was not until that time that the writings needed to be formally identified, as the authors were known to the public as a matter of common knowledge. Early church documents identify that Luke was a student of Paul. While Luke would not have been an eyewitness to the Gospel events, he clearly states at the beginning of his Gospel that his goal is to write a historical account of Jesus based on the eyewitness testimony. The early church leaders identify Mark's gospel as the eyewitness testimony of Peter who was one of Jesus' closest disciples, and they identify Matthew and John as Gospel writers who were disciples of Jesus. Non-Christian scholars essentially dispute all of these arguments, saying these arguments are all conjecture and that there is very little evidence of who actually wrote the Gospel accounts.[40]

My personal assessment of reliability: I really have no idea how to assess this one either, and feel like the arguments are 50/50.

Natalie's Points: 0

Internal Test #3: Contradictions

The contradiction test looks at the independent sources recording the events and looks to find any contradictions between the accounts. If the various sources contradict each other, it is an indication that the documents are less likely to be historically reliable. There is, however, a bit of a rub with this test. If the individual accounts are too similar, historians may conclude that the authors colluded to ensure they had "the same story," which would also be an indicator that they are less likely to be historically reliable.

Debate: Are there significant contradictions between the Gospel accounts and letters of Paul that would lead historians to question their historical reliability?

It seems to me there is a great deal of debate as to what actually constitutes a "contradiction" between the Gospel writings. Non-Christian scholars contend there are many contradictions between the Gospel narratives which serve to discredit their historical reliability. Here is a quick example: The Gospel of Matthew records that following the birth of Jesus, Mary and Joseph had to flee to Egypt to escape King Herod's decree to kill all baby boys in the region. The Gospel of Luke, on the other hand, documents that Mary and Joseph traveled to Jerusalem to dedicate Jesus at the temple according to Jewish customs. Critics argue it is simply not possible for both of these events to have taken place right after the birth of Jesus; therefore, this presents an unreconcilable contradiction.

Christian scholars, on the other hand, argue that when analyzing verses such as these the reader cannot make assumptions about the chronology of the events or reasons why one author may have omitted certain aspects of the account. They argue it is completely reasonable to conclude that these events both occurred just during different time periods and that one author reported on different details than the other.[41]

My personal assessment of reliability: This one left me feeling really confused. There were other examples of contradictions similar to this one that, in my opinion, present a bit of challenge to the Gospel's historical reliability. For that reason, I cannot award a point for reliability on this test either.

Natalie's Points: 0

Internal Test #4:
Criterion of Embarrassment

Historians often contend that when an author includes information that is potentially embarrassing or goes against their own self-interest it is more likely the account is historically reliable. The logic on this one is that if you are going to make up a story or lie, you are far more likely to paint yourself in a more positive light.

Debate. Do the writings of the New Testament present any scenarios that could be considered embarrassing to the author or to the followers of Jesus?

Christian scholars argue there are actually several things in the Gospels that could be considered embarrassing to the authors and to the followers of Jesus in general. Here are just a few examples. Jesus' disciple Peter was supposedly one of his most faithful and bold followers. After Jesus was arrested, the Gospels describe a situation where Peter denied even knowing Jesus because he feared for his own safety. The Gospel writers, especially Peter, would be hesitant to share this account as it would portray the followers of Jesus as afraid and unwilling to defend him.

Christian scholars argue that one of the most embarrassing details presented in the writings about Jesus is the fact that the guy they claimed was the Jewish messiah and the Son of God, died a humiliating death on a Roman cross. This was completely contrary to what Jews had anticipated concerning the prophesied Jewish Messiah. They were under the impression that the Messiah would be a great heroic and gallant leader who would free Israel from the bonds of oppression. Instead, Jesus taught that the ways of his kingdom were different than the ways of the world and that his sacrifice would free them from the bonds of sin, versus the oppression of worldly governments.[42]

Non-Christian scholars tend to dismiss the criterion-of-embarrassment test altogether, suggesting the test is not a good assessment of historical reliability.

My personal assessment of reliability. It does seem to me that the authors of these texts presented many details that essentially put themselves and

Jesus in a negative light. We will see a little later that their claims about Jesus even put them at great risk, as many were persecuted and even killed for their beliefs. It does not appear there would have been any motive for lying in this situation as it would not serve to benefit them in any way. I will give this test a half point as being a possible indicator of reliability.

Natalie's Points: +.5

While there are other internal tests, these few give us a fairly good indication of the types of questions they look at to assess the reliability of the historical writings. My total score for the internal test section is 1 out of 4. While I am not rushing to the conclusion that the Gospels and letters of Paul are historically unreliable at this point, it is my opinion that they do not measure up very strongly when applied to the internal tests. Let's see how they do in the other two categories.

Bibliographical Tests

The next set of tests used to gauge historical reliability is what historians collectively refer to as bibliographical tests. While internal tests focus on the author and content of the documents, bibliographical tests focus on the transmission of the content over time. We learned earlier that we do not currently have any of the original documents, as they likely deteriorated long ago. During this period of time when there was a need for additional copies of important texts, it had to be hand-copied. There was a group of specially trained people, called scribes, that would copy the text. This group of people underwent intense training to ensure that the copy, which they called a manuscript, reflected the original text as closely as possible. Inevitably, however, there were mistakes made and on occasion scribes would purposefully make changes to the text to further a particular political or religious agenda. The bibliographical tests are designed to assess the manuscript copies and determine whether or not they reliably convey the intent of the original writings.

Bibliographical Test #1:
Number of Manuscripts

The more manuscripts (handwritten copies) of the text that are available to historians today, the better opportunity they have to ascertain what the original document likely said. This seems rather counterintuitive, as the more copies that are available, the more differences can be found between the various copies. The key to this test is, the more the better.

Debate: Is there a sufficient number of remaining manuscripts to allow historians to determine whether or not these copies accurately and reliably reflect the language of the original document?

Let me start out by giving you statistics on the number of manuscript copies historians have to work with. Keep in mind that a manuscript can be just a small fragment of a copy or the entire text. There is currently a total of nearly 25,000 New Testament manuscripts which includes approximately 5,800 manuscripts written in Greek (believed to be the original language of the New Testament documents) and another 19,000 manuscripts written in languages such as Latin, Coptic, Syriac, and Aramaic. This number continues to grow as archaeologists make additional discoveries. The number of New Testament manuscripts far exceeds the number of manuscripts for any other writing in antiquity.[43] Other works of antiquity have far fewer manuscript copies available today. For example, there are about 1,800 remaining manuscript copies of Homer's *Iliad* and about 251 remaining manuscripts of Caesar's *Gallic Wars*.[44]

My personal assessment of reliability: Even non-Christian scholars do not debate the fact that there is an absolute abundance of New Testament manuscripts available for study. I will definitely give this one a point as an indicator of historical reliability.

Natalie's Points: +1

Bibliographical Test #2:
Date of Earliest Manuscripts

The next important thing to determine is the time gap that exists between the original document and the earliest known manuscript. It is important to have a strong chain of evidence between the original and the manuscript copies to ensure the text had not changed during that time. The greater the time gap between those two dates, the less likely the manuscript is to be historically reliable.

Debate: Does the time gap between the original writings of the Gospels and letters of Paul and the earliest known manuscript indicate they are more or less likely to be historically reliable?

I have included another simple chart to indicate the approximate time gaps between the original Gospels and letters of Paul and the earliest known manuscripts. Keep in mind these are approximations, since historians and scholars are only able to give approximate dates for both the originals and the age of existing manuscripts.

Writing/ Approximate time gap between original and earliest known manuscript[45]
Gospel of John/ Max 55 years
Gospel of Matthew/ Max 120 years
Gospel of Mark/ Max 184 years
Gospel of Luke/ Max 140 years
Letters of Paul/ Max 151 years

Again, it is important to have some perspective on how these compare to other writings from antiquity. Most have significantly higher gaps of time between the dates of the original writings and the dates of the earliest known manuscripts. For example, Homer's *Iliad* has a gap of about four hundred years and Caesar's *Gallic Wars* has about a 950-year time gap.[46]

My personal assessment of reliability: While the New Testament manuscripts rate better in this area than any other writing of ancient times, it still causes me some concern. Most of the earliest manuscripts are very small fragments. The earliest complete manuscript of the New Testament, known as Codex Vaticanus, was believed to have been written sometime between 325–350 CE. While small fragments do present valuable evidence for reliability, the fact that that the earliest complete manuscript is more than two hundred years later than the original leaves me wondering what happened during that time period. For this reason, I am giving it only half a point.

Natalie's Points: +.5

Bibliographical Test #3:
Manuscript Variants

Now that we have established how many manuscript copies historians have and the dates of the earliest existing manuscripts, let's take a look at the very important variants test. Earlier we applied what is called the contradictions test. That test looked specifically at contradictions or variations between the Gospel writers. The question in that test was whether Matthew, Mark, Luke, or John were telling different versions of the stories. Now we are going to be looking at differences or variants found between the surviving manuscript copies. Any variations between the copies is an indication that the text had somehow been changed over the years. In other words, the more differences there are found between the copies, the less likely the integrity of the original text had been preserved and the less historically reliable it is likely to be.

Debate: Do the differences found between the New Testament manuscripts present evidence that significant changes have occurred in the text, making them historically unreliable?

Both non-Christian and Christian scholars agree that there are thousands of variations between the remaining manuscript copies of the Gospels. To be fair, part of the reason scholars can find so many variations is because there are so many manuscripts to compare! These variations include everything from differences in punctuation, spelling, and word order, which are relatively minor and don't affect the meaning of the text; to significant differences that potentially bring into question important doctrines of the faith.

Christian scholars contend that the minor differences account for as much as 99.5% of the differences found between the manuscripts. They do acknowledge that about .5% of the differences are significant, but argue that they do not affect or change any core Christian beliefs.[47]

While non-Christian scholars agree that the number of meaningful variants are very small, they argue that the variants naturally bring into question the integrity of the manuscripts and whether or not they accurately reflect the original text. Here is an example that caught my attention, since this Gospel story had always been very meaningful to me: In the Gospel of John, verses 7:53–8:11, an angry mob of people had gathered to stone to death a woman who had been caught in the act of adultery. Jesus stepped in and boldly said, don't throw a stone at this woman unless you yourself are sinless. The mob then backs down, and Jesus lovingly tells the woman to go live a good and sinless life. It turns out that this story was likely not in the original Gospel text and was likely added somewhere in the copying process. It is possible that it happened and was simply added to the Gospel later as it had been inadvertently left out, but no one can be sure. The fact remains: these kinds of variants, as limited as they are, can bring into question the historicity and reliability of the text.[48]

My personal assessment of reliability: I do agree that differences between the text are worth noting and are certainly reminders of how susceptible these writings were to inadvertent or purposeful changes. I did not find the majority of differences to be overwhelmingly significant. However, since there were some that caused me a bit of concern, I will give the variants test a half a point for likelihood of reliability.

Natalie's points: +.5

In my opinion, the Gospels fared a bit better in terms of the bibliographic test. I have scored it a total of 2 out of 3 points as evidence of historical reliability. Before reaching a final conclusion on the topic, let's take a look at the final test.

External Tests

The final set of tests historians use to assess historical reliability is what they collectively refer to as the external tests. The external tests examine non-Christian sources that confirm or contradict the events recorded in the Gospels and letters written by Paul. The more external sources there are to corroborate the accounts recorded in these documents, the more likely they are to be historically reliable and vice versa. External sources can include non-New Testament writings, government records, and archaeological evidence.

External Test #1: Non-Christian Sources

There are many different sources of non-Christian writings that reference events or claims made in the Gospels and letters of Paul. Historians will actually give additional historicity credits when the external source is considered an enemy or hostile to the Christian movement, as they would typically be less likely to promote the agenda of someone they considered to be an enemy. Here are some of the main external writings that mention Jesus. For the most part, there is not a lot of debate between Christian and non-Christian scholars concerning these writings, but I will mention them when relevant.

The writings of Josephus: Josephus was a Jewish historian writing the history of the Jews during and after the time of Jesus. There is much debate over what the original writings of Josephus actually said, as it is believed that Christians may have inserted text into these writings to make them appear more favorable to the Christian cause. Most scholars would agree that at the very least, the writings of Josephus confirm the following facts:

- that Jesus performed startling deeds;
- that many Jews and Gentiles followed him;
- that Pilate condemned him to death on a cross;
- that those who loved him continued to follow his teachings after his death; and
- that James, the brother of Jesus, became the leader of the Christian church and was eventually killed because of what he believed.[49]

The writings of Tacitus: Tacitus was a Roman historian who wrote about the history of first-century Rome. His writings corroborate the following facts of the Gospels:

- that Jesus was executed under Pontius Pilate during the reign of Tiberius Caesar and suffered the extreme penalty of crucifixion; and
- that Christians were willing to be tortured and die for their beliefs about Jesus.[50]

The Jewish Talmud: Remember that the Jewish Talmud documents Jewish law and provides guidance from Jewish rabbis. There is some debate between Christian and non-Christian scholars as to whether or not certain verses of the Talmud actually refer to Jesus. At the very least the Talmud confirms the following facts:

- that Jesus practiced "magic" and "sorcery" which led Israel astray;
- that Jesus was hung on the eve of Passover; and
- at least five of Jesus' disciples are identified.[51]

Lucian of Samosota: Lucian was a second-century Greek satirist (comedian). While his comments about Jesus were very negative, they did confirm a couple facts:

- Christians worshiped Jesus who was crucified; and

- Christians taught that they were all brothers, and that Greeks should deny the gods of Greece and worship the crucified sage (wise man).[52]

My personal assessment of reliability: While I did not include all the non-biblical writings about Jesus here, I must admit that I was surprised to see there were not more external writings about Jesus. In fact, many non-Christian scholars list this as a concern for the reliability of the Gospels. It did occur to me that this could be another example of our twenty-first-century lenses. Today, news spreads quickly through social media and new outlets. As we know, that was not the case in the first century when most people did not even know how to read or write. In my opinion, the fact that there are several references to Jesus in these ancient writings and that they verify facts found in in the Gospels (although in a notably different light) serves as a strong indicator of historical reliability of the Gospel accounts.

Natalie's Points: +1

External Test #2:
Archaeological Evidence

Archaeology is the study of human history accomplished by excavating various sites in search of artifacts from the past. These artifacts give archaeologists and historians insight about past human behavior and how societies developed. Archaeological discoveries can also serve to confirm or discredit details found in ancient documents. There have been many archaeological discoveries that serve to confirm people and places mentioned in the New Testament writings. While none of them provide absolute assurance that the accounts are correct, they do serve as an indicator that the Gospels and letters of Paul are historically reliable. There seems to me to be very little debate between scholars concerning this evidence.[53] Here are just a few of the more notable archaeological discoveries relevant to these texts.

- *Ossuary box of James:* An ossuary box (a box containing the bones of the deceased) was found near Jerusalem in 2002 with an inscription reading, *"James, Son of Joseph, Brother of Jesus."* This is believed to be an authentic inscription dating back to the first century, and supports New Testament reference to the fact that Jesus had a brother named James.

- *Crucifixion victim:* In 1968 an archaeologist discovered the partial remains of a crucifixion victim, including the victim's left heel bone containing the seven-inch nail which had been driven through his foot. This confirms the Gospel accounts that described the methods used to crucify Jesus.

- *Evidence for the first-century city of Nazareth:* Historians used to question whether the city of Nazareth, where the Gospels report that Jesus lived as a child, actually existed in the first century. Recently archaeologists have found evidence of first-century homes in the area of Nazareth, which confirms the Gospel accounts.

- *Pontius Pilate stone:* In 1961 an inscription was found confirming that Pilate was the political ruler in the land of Judea as a "prefect." This inscription has been found to be authentic and dates back between 26 and 37 CE, which would be consistent with the accounts of the Gospels stating that Pilate sentenced Jesus to be crucified.

- *The tomb of Caiaphas:* In 1992 the tomb of the high priest Caiaphas, who was noted in the Gospels as the priest who presided over the trial of Jesus, was discovered on the outskirts of Jerusalem.

- *Dead Sea Scrolls:* Beginning in 1946 a series of ancient documents were discovered in caves in an area known as Qumran, located near the Dead Sea in Israel. There they discovered 220 scrolls containing portions of the Hebrew Bible. Prior to the Qumran discovery the oldest known copy of the Hebrew Bible dated back to about 950 CE. The discovery of the Dead Sea scrolls—which, by the way, are remarkably consistent with the text of today's Hebrew Bible—brought a whole new level of historical reliability to the Jewish scriptures. Carbon testing dates the oldest scroll to about 150 BCE. While the scrolls do not provide much in terms of evidence to support the New Testament writings, they do corroborate what Jesus taught about the Hebrew Bible, as he often quoted it and spoke about Jewish prophets from the past.

My personal assessment of reliability: Of everything I have studied so far, this topic was the most fun for me. I was so fascinated by it that I took a trip to Israel to actually see some of these artifacts and to experience the environment, terrain, and culture. There is no doubt in my mind that archaeological discoveries confirm details of the Gospels and letters of Paul. That does not necessarily prove anything other than to say the authors accurately reported on many aspects of life in the first century, as well as on many details of places and political figures of the time. I will definitely give this one a point for reliability.

Natalie's Points: +1

The external test provided me with the most powerful evidence concerning the historical reliability of the Gospels I have seen so far. Perhaps it is the fact that it presents the most objective evidence between the three tests. I gave the Gospels a strong 2 out of 2 when applied against the external tests.

Conclusion

While we did not look at every historical methodology test historians and scholars use to assess the historicity of the Gospels and letters of Paul, this gives us a good idea of how they fare. So, what does all of this mean? Did any of it give us any insight or bring us any closer to definitively determining whether or not the Christian claims about God are accurate—and ultimately gaining an understanding of who the designer of the universe is?

My answer would have to be: I don't think so. There were certainly some places where the writings fared well when applied to the tests, but others where they did not. According to my calculations out of the 9 possible points in our informal poll, I only awarded 5 total points on the side of historical reliability. That essentially results in a little better than 50–50 odds of historical reliability, which is not all that convincing.

Studying these tests did provide me with enough evidence to support at least one conclusion: there certainly seems to be ample evidence to conclude, beyond a reasonable doubt, that there actually was a guy named Jesus who lived during the first century in Israel. I have heard some skeptics throw out the claim that it cannot be definitively proven that Jesus actually even existed, contending that he was nothing more than a myth or legend. The evidence, at least in my mind, does not support that statement in any way. Even Bart Ehrman, who is a New Testament scholar identifying as an atheist, said this about Jesus: "There is no scholar in any college or university who teaches classics, ancient history, new testament, early Christianity who doubts that Jesus existed. . . . Early and independent sources indicate that Jesus certainly existed."[54] Here is a tip: if you are ever tempted to throw out the fact that Jesus never existed during the next philosophical debate with your buddy, I would advise you to do some further research to back up your claim, in order to prevent looking quite silly.

With all of this said, I believe I find myself undecided. In the legal field we refer to this as a "hung jury." I am just not able to make a decision based on this evidence. I still find myself asking the question: Who is this intelligent designer, God?

Chapter 9

JUST KEEP DIGGING

Years ago, when my kids and I were struggling in a particular situation, we would repeat the words of the wise and witty Dory from the movie *Finding Nemo*: "Just keep swimming, just keep swimming." As we repeated that together, we often found a way to laugh our way through difficult situations and keep moving forward.

I will be honest: at this point in my research it would be more accurate to describe myself as frantically flailing rather than swimming! I have spent months reviewing these historical methodologies and don't feel it got me much closer to finding an answer to my question. I had been able to use science to help me reach the conclusion that there is an intelligent force at work behind the scenes in our universe, but is it even possible to objectively determine the nature and identity of that force? All I can say is, "Just keep swimming, just keep swimming!"

I decided I needed to get back to something a little more familiar. Historical methodologies are great and all, but I felt the need to do some good old-fashioned legal fact analysis. When studying the existence of an intelligent designer, we established a list of facts which could be supported by evidence and generally accepted by both sides of the debate. Once we had that list of facts, we were able to use them to reach a final decision in the case based on logical and reasoned inference. Perhaps the next step with the issue in front of us is to build a similar set of facts to see if we can get any closer to an answer. It is worth a try.

Minimal Facts

Aaaaaahhhhhh! (That represents me screaming.) It does not happen often, but sometimes you are lucky enough to find gold. As I began to look for a way to assemble a group of facts that both sides of the debate would agree to, I discovered the work had already been done for me! I found an argument called the "minimal facts" approach, first introduced by a Christian historian named Gary Habermas.

Habermas holds PhDs in both history and the philosophy of religion. He argues there are a handful of facts that the majority of New Testament scholars, whether Christian or non-Christian, agree can be considered historically reliable. He uses two criteria to establish his list of facts. First, the facts must be supported by evidence which strongly indicates historical reliability according to historical method tests we just studied. Second, a large majority—like 90% percent—of New Testament scholars, whether Christian or non-Christian, must agree that the facts are historically reliable.[55] Now we are swimming!

Before we dive into these facts, I would like to take a minute to talk about the apostle Paul. We have already referenced some of his letters in the New Testament, but I want to make sure to explain why he is such an important resource as we study the historicity of Jesus. Paul is unique in the sense that he never met Jesus during his lifetime. After the death of Jesus, Saul, as he was known at the time, was actually a Jewish leader who persecuted Christians and sought to suppress the early growing movement. He claims that Jesus appeared to him after he was knocked off of his horse by a blinding light while traveling to the city of Damascus. Later, changing his name to Paul, he claimed that this event resulted in his conversion to Christianity. He went on to become one of the most influential people in the early Christian church. As we walk through the "minimal facts," we will see how Paul's letters play an important role in Christian claims.

As we look at each of these minimal facts, we will examine the historical evidence for reliability based on the historical methodologies and focus on the opinions of non-Christian scholars who conclude these facts are historically reliable. I will also again be including my own informal point system to help me personally assess the historical reliability of these facts.

Minimal Fact #1:
Jesus Died by Crucifixion

Historical Evidence:

- *Early sources*—Since some scholars do not consider the Gospels themselves to be early sources, we will not include them as early sources corroborating the death of Jesus by crucifixion. Very few scholars, however, would deny that Paul's letters constitute early sources as they were actually written before the Gospels. Paul's first letter to the Corinthians was written in about 55 CE and references the crucifixion and death of Jesus. That dates attestation to this fact as early as twenty-five years after Jesus died on the cross. Scholars believe that in his letter to the Corinthians, Paul was actually making reference to an existing creed which proclaimed the core Christian beliefs. That, in effect, means that the fact Jesus died by crucifixion was an established Christian belief sometime prior to 55 CE. We will talk more about the significance of this creed a little later. The important thing to note is that the early reporting of this fact indicates historical reliability and makes it far less likely to be a false claim, myth, or legend that developed over time.[56]

- *Non-Christian sources*—As we saw earlier, if non-Christian sources verify a fact it is more likely to be historically reliable. There are at the very least four non-Christian writings that record the death of Jesus by crucifixion including Josephus, Tacitus, Lucian, and the Jewish Talmud. A few of these can also be considered hostile sources, which serves as an even stronger indicator for historical reliability.

- *Archaeological evidence*—We saw earlier that the heelbone of a crucifixion victim, from roughly the same time period as Jesus, was discovered in an archaeological dig near Jerusalem. This served to confirm that some of the reported details about the crucifixion of Jesus were accurate, which is an indicator of historical reliability.

Non-Christian scholars' opinions on the historicity of this fact:

- John Dominic Crossan is a New Testament scholar and critic of the Bible's historical reliability. He is quoted as saying, "Jesus' death by crucifixion under Pontius Pilate is as sure as anything historical can ever be."

- Gerd Lüdemann, a German New Testament scholar and atheist, said, "Jesus' death as a consequence of crucifixion is indisputable."[57]

- Bart Ehrman, a New Testament scholar and Bible critic, states, "There are a few things we can say with virtual certainty about Jesus. He was a Jewish preacher from rural Galilee who made the fateful trip to Jerusalem and was crucified by the Roman governor Pontius Pilate."[58]

My personal assessment of reliability: The fact that Jesus died as a result of crucifixion is very well attested and supported by the historical tests. I can find very little reason to doubt this fact is historically reliable.

Natalie's Points: +1

Minimal Fact #2:
Jesus' Tomb Was Found Empty

Historical evidence:

- *Nonbiblical sources*—In a letter written in 165 CE, a Christian by the name of Justin Martyr reported that there was a letter circulating in the Jewish community reporting that the body of Jesus had been stolen from the tomb. Reports that Jews claim the body was stolen serve to confirm the fact that the tomb was empty.[59]

- *Embarrassment*—The Gospel accounts report that women followers of Jesus were going to the tomb to anoint Jesus' body with oil and spices when they discovered the tomb was empty. It is well-established fact that at this time in history, Jews considered the testimony of women to be completely unreliable. Scholars argue that if the empty tomb story was fabricated the authors would never have reported that women discovered it. If the story was fabricated, it would have made far more sense to report that men found it. Therefore, this report indicates the fact is historically reliable.[60]

Non-Christian scholars' opinions on the historicity of this fact:

This is the one fact that does not get a 90% acceptance rate by non-Christian scholars. Research shows that about 75% of non-Christian scholars would agree that this fact is historically reliable. Many scholars who deny the empty tomb argue that Jesus was likely never buried in a tomb, as the custom at the time would never have permitted a criminal to have a proper burial. They therefore argue that if Jesus was never buried in a tomb, it could not be found empty.[61]

- Michael Grant, a secular historian writes, "If we apply the same criteria that we would apply to other ancient literary sources, the evidence is firm and plausible enough to necessitate the conclusion that the tomb was, indeed, found empty."[62]

- Bart Ehrman: "It seems much more likely that, at least with the traditions involving the empty tomb, we are dealing with something actually rooted in history."[63]

My personal assessment of reliability: While the fact seems to pass historical reliability testing, it is not as strongly supported by non-Christian scholars. For that reason, I will give it half a point for reliability.

Natalie's Points: +.5

Minimal Fact #3:
The Disciples of Jesus Sincerely Believed They Saw Jesus Alive Again after His Death and Drastically Changed Their Behavior Despite Great Risk

(Keep in mind this fact is not confirming that Jesus appeared alive again after his death—just that people sincerely believed they saw him again.)

Historical evidence:

- *Early sources*—Paul's letters are again considered one of the earliest written sources that record the appearance of Jesus after his death. In 1 Corinthians 15, Paul reports that Jesus appeared to Peter, the rest of the twelve disciples, to a group of five hundred people, to James, to another group of followers, and then at last to him. These appearances by Jesus would have also been part of the early creed we have mentioned.

- *Criterion of embarrassment*—Immediately following Jesus' death, the Gospels record that the disciples hid because they feared they would be killed as well. Following the reported appearances, the disciples came out of hiding and began to boldly proclaim the message of Jesus. Those reports serve as evidence that the disciples witnessed and experienced something dramatic enough to overcome their fear. While this evidence cannot prove they actually saw the risen Jesus, it does support the fact that they sincerely thought they did.

- *Non-Christian sources*—There are no non-Christian sources to my knowledge who report that Jesus actually appeared alive again after his death. Josephus, Tacitus, Suetonius, and others wrote about the persecution of Christians, which they endured because of their beliefs. Again, this does not serve as proof that Jesus appeared to the disciples after his death, but it does support the fact that the disciples experienced something that gave them the courage and conviction to proclaim their beliefs despite the risk of persecution and martyrdom.

- *Author bias and motives*—We did not review this test when we looked at the historical methodologies. This test essentially looks for any biases or motives the disciples would have had to lie about the appearances of Jesus after his death. There are no reports that the disciples gained anything financially, politically, or socially as a result of these claims. In fact, what is recorded suggests the complete opposite: they were willing to give up everything they had, to suffer, and even to die for what they believed to be true. It is also important to note that their willingness to suffer and die was based on their firsthand knowledge of what they knew to be true, not simply on what someone else told them to believe. This evidence serves as strong support of the fact that the disciples sincerely believed they saw Jesus again after his death.

- *Eyewitness testimony*—Since many scholars do not feel there is enough evidence to confidently identify the authors of the Gospels, they cannot be considered to be eyewitness testimony. Paul, however, can be considered an eyewitness to the post-death appearance of Jesus. He states in his first letter to the Corinthians that the risen Jesus appeared to him, which makes him an eyewitness to that event and adds historical reliability to this fact.[64]

Non-Christian scholars' opinions on the historicity of this fact:

- Gerd Lüdemann: "It may be taken as historically certain that Peter and the disciples had experiences after Jesus' death in which Jesus appeared to them as the risen Christ."[65]

- Bart Ehrman: "It is a historical fact that some of Jesus' followers came to believe that he had been risen from the dead soon after his execution."[66]

- Pinchas Lapide, a Jewish historian, states, "This does not prove that the resurrection is true. But it shows the depth of the apostles' convictions. They were not liars. They truly believed Jesus rose from the grave and were willing to give their lives for it."

- Robert Funk, who founded the Jesus Seminar and questioned the historical reliability of the Gospels, said, "The disciples thought they had witnessed Jesus' appearances, which, however they are explained, is a fact upon which both believers and unbelievers may agree."

- Paula Fredrickson, a liberal scholar, states, "If Jesus had died and stayed dead, they would have either given up on the movement, or they would have found another messiah. Something extraordinary happened to convince them that Jesus was the messiah."[67]

My personal assessment of reliability: The fact that Jesus' followers witnessed his brutal death and were so confident that they saw him alive again that they made radical and bold changes despite the risk of persecution make this fact very historically reliable. It seems this fact is also well accepted by non-Christian skeptical scholars. I feel confident in relying on this fact as an indicator of historical reliability.

Natalie's Points: +1

Minimal Fact #4:
Previous Nonbelievers Converted to Christianity, Following
What They Believed to Be the Resurrection of Jesus
(e.g., Paul, and James the brother of Jesus)

Historical Evidence:

- *Early sources:*
  - Paul concerning James—In Paul's first letter to the Corinthians he reports meeting with James, the brother of Jesus, who had become a leader in the Jerusalem church. This is significant because as we will see, prior to Jesus' death his brother James had accused Jesus of being crazy.
  - Paul's references to himself—In his letter to the Galatians, Paul talks about his previous attempts to destroy the movement started by Jesus. In his letters to the Philippians, Paul speaks of participating in the stoning death of Stephen, one of the early church leaders. Despite his earlier views, Paul went on to become one of the most important leaders of the Christian movement after the death of Jesus.
- *Criterion of embarrassment*—The Gospel of Mark mentions that Jesus' brothers at one point during his life thought he was crazy and tried to convince him to come back home. This fact would likely be a source of embarrassment to Jesus' followers, which indicates the report is more likely to be historically reliable.
- *Non-Christian sources*—The Jewish historian Josephus writes that James the brother of Jesus was put to death by stoning for breaking the Jewish law, confirming that James at some point had an experience that converted him from a Jesus-skeptic to a Jesus-believer.

Non-Christian scholars' opinions on the historicity of this fact:

- Bart Ehrman: "That Jesus' followers (and later Paul) had resurrection experiences is, in my judgment, a fact. What the reality is that gave rise to the experiences I do not know."[68]

- Pinchas Lapide: "[T]he apostles were willing to suffer for their faith. This is certainly true of Paul, who recounts the suffering he endured, which included being whipped, beaten, stoned, shipwrecked, near starvation and in danger from various people and places."[69]

My personal assessment of reliability: The fact that both Paul and James were reported as being strongly opposed and resistant to the claims of Jesus during his lifetime and later took leadership positions in the early church indicates that the conversion of these two previous skeptics were historically reliable.

Natalie's Points: +1

Minimal Fact #5:
There Was a Very Early Creed Declaring Christian Beliefs

I will need to set some preliminary context on this one before we get started. Hang in there with me, as this can be a bit confusing but also very important. Scholars commonly acknowledge that Paul's letters were the earliest writings about Jesus, actually written before the Gospels themselves. Paul presumably wrote his letters roughly twenty-five to thirty years after the death of Jesus. An important question to consider is: What did Christians practice and believe prior to the writings of Paul? Paul's first letter to the Corinthians might shed some light on this question:

For what I received I passed on to you as of first importance: that Christ died for our sins according to the Scriptures, that he was buried, that he was raised on the third day according to the

Scriptures, and that he appeared to Cephas (Peter), and then to the Twelve. After that, he appeared to more than five hundred of the brothers and sisters at the same time, most of whom are still living, though some have fallen asleep. Then he appeared to James, then to all the apostles, and last of all he appeared to me also, as to one untimely born. (1 Corinthians 15:3–8)

The words Paul uses to describe what he received and passed on, in the original Greek and Aramaic language, specifically refer to the process of delivering and passing on tradition. During ancient times the vast majority of people could not read or write; therefore, oral tradition was extremely common and important. It was the way in which people preserved and transmitted history, events, and beliefs from one generation to the next. Because memorizing oral traditions was challenging and time-consuming, many cultures developed what they called "creeds." Creeds were short, formalized statements that summarized beliefs and were easy for the average Joe to remember. Many scholars and historians believe that the early Christians relied on oral tradition to preserve the details of the events that took place during the ministry of Jesus and established a creed which they used to both preserve and proclaim their core beliefs.

While many of us wearing our twenty-first century lenses may be skeptical about the reliability of oral traditions, in many ways they are considered as historically important as written documentation. The preservation and transmission of oral tradition was taken very seriously by past cultures. Often there were specifically trained people to teach the oral tradition, and strict rules and guidelines about how it was transmitted. Great care was taken to ensure that stories and accounts were transmitted accurately. Narratives and stories were often arranged and performed as songs, dances, poems, or plays to make them easier to remember. While many in the twenty-first century quickly question the reliability of oral traditions, historians and scholars have learned they are valuable evidence of the past. Oral tradition is considered even more reliable when it can be used in conjunction with corroborating written material.[70]

With that background in mind, let's take a look at the evidence suggesting there was early Christian oral tradition in the form of a creed.

Historical evidence:

- *Early sources*—As we discussed above in Paul's first letter to the Corinthians, written about twenty-five years after Jesus died on the cross, he mentions that he was given information in the form of tradition that he was passing on to them. In several of Paul's other letters, he documents his travels. When creating a timeline of these travels, we can determine that he would likely have gotten this creed during his visit to Jerusalem in 35 CE when he spent time with Peter and James. That necessarily means that the creed had to have been in existence prior to 35 CE, which puts it a maximum of five years after Jesus died on the cross. Many scholars would argue that this creed was likely developed shortly after the death of Jesus on the cross.[71]

Non-Christian scholars' opinions on the historicity of this fact:

- Gerd Lüdemann: "[T]he elements in the tradition are to be dated to the first two years after the crucifixion of Jesus . . . not later than three years."
- Robert Funk: "The conviction that Jesus had risen from the dead had already taken root by the time Paul was converted about 33 CE."
- Michael Goulder, an atheist scholar, said about the creed, "It goes back at least to what Paul was taught when he was converted, a couple years after the crucifixion."[72]

My personal assessment of reliability: The evidence of this oral Christian creed seems very strong to me. Because evidence of this creed was documented a maximum of five years after the death of Jesus, its historicity is even more likely. Because of this—in addition to the fact that this creed is further evidence by both the Gospels and even non-Christian writings—I find it to be a historically reliable representation of what the very early Christian church believed about Jesus.

Natalie's Points: +1

That is a score of 4.5 out of 5. That certainly gives me more to think about!

Chapter 10

TIME FOR A DECISION

I don't know about you, but I can't take anymore! Like science, history is beginning to numb my brain and I am afraid it could be permanent. Thanks for hanging in there with me and digging into another very deep and difficult subject. I think we now have enough information to make an educated and informed decision for ourselves.

As I have stated many times before, it is important to note that I have only scratched the surface of New Testament historical study. There is far more than I was able to include here. I did my best to include what I found to be the leading arguments on each side of the debate and to present them as succinctly and accurately as possible. If you still find yourself struggling with any of the points we studied, I would encourage you to do some further internet recon in an effort to get a better understanding. If you find anything interesting, please let me know!

I will again share my own personal analysis and decision on these issues with you, but encourage and expect that you will take the time to weigh the evidence for yourself and make your own decision. As always, the most important thing is that you take the time to understand what you believe and why you believe it, rather than simply relying only on what someone else has told you to believe.

Evidence, Facts, and Conclusions

We started this journey by asking the question: What is the nature of the intelligent designer responsible for the creation of DNA, the code for life? It seems that the only option for defining who that intelligent designer might be is in the context of religion. Religion, throughout the course of human history, has typically defined this intelligent life-giving force as God. In an attempt to gain insight into who God is, we studied the beliefs of the major world religions. While that study proved to be very interesting and educational, it could not provide us with objective evidence about the nature and identity of God. The Christian's claim about Jesus presented us with an opportunity to find the objective evidence we were looking for. Christians claim that God came to Earth as the person of Jesus of Nazareth. That means they are claiming that God inserted himself into the course of human history. The question is, can the study of history help us reach a conclusion about the nature and identity of God?

After applying the historical methodologies to the Gospel writings and letters of Paul, I personally could not find enough evidence to make a decision. We then turned to the fact-based strategy we had used in our earlier scientific research. It turned out the work had been done for us in an argument referred to as the minimal facts approach. We focused on five facts about Jesus; we looked at the historical evidence to support those facts and reactions from non-Christian historians and scholars about the historicity of each fact; and found these facts to be well supported and virtually unquestioned as historically reliable:

- Jesus died by crucifixion.
- Jesus' tomb was found empty.
- The disciples of Jesus sincerely believed they saw Jesus alive again after his death, and drastically changed their behavior despite great risk.

- Previous nonbelievers converted to Christianity, following what they believed to be the resurrection of Jesus.

- There was a very early creed declaring Christian beliefs.

The next step in the process is to determine whether these facts establish a strong inference (bridge) to one side of the debate or the other. Christian scholars and historians, of course, claim that Jesus died and resurrected from the dead, while non-Christian scholars and historians contend these claims were exaggerated and a result of legend.

Struggling a bit to link the facts to an ultimate conclusion, I ran across a strategy proposed by Christian historians and scholars to help assess the minimal facts. They propose exploring and assessing all possible explanations for the facts and reaching a conclusion based on the most reasonable and logical inference. Let's take a look to see if this strategy can help us reach a decision.

If the evidence supports the fact that Jesus died by crucifixion, what other theories might explain the fact that the tomb he had been buried in was found empty? Some non-Christian scholars and historians propose what they call "swoon theory." The theory suggests that Jesus did not actually die on the cross, but perhaps lost consciousness to the point of having no detectable pulse. Sometime after he was placed in the tomb, he regained consciousness and was able to escape from the tomb.[73] As I considered and studied the possibility of this theory it did not seem logical to me given the fact that just days after Jesus' supposed death he appeared to his disciples. Jesus had been violently beaten and crucified: wouldn't he still have been a bloody, battered mess?

I did some research on Roman scourging and crucifixion. It is reported that the Romans scourged Jesus before they nailed him to the cross. Historical evidence suggests that when the Romans scourged (whipped) their victim they used a device called a *flagrum*—a whip with multiple straps of leather holding heavy pieces of metal and sharp objects. It was designed to rip the victim's flesh open. The Jewish historian Josephus reported that flagellation often left the victim's innards exposed.

It was after this that the Romans would have nailed Jesus to the cross, driving seven-inch metal spikes into his hands and feet. He was then left there to hang for several hours in the scorching sun without water. Finally, to ensure he was dead, the Roman soldiers thrust a spear through his side, at which point it was recorded that blood and water flowed from his body. We know today that the presence of water with the blood would have indicated he had died. I apologize for being so graphic, but it is to make this point: it is highly unlikely that Jesus did not actually die on the cross.[74] Knowing this, even if Jesus did not actually die, he would have appeared to the disciples in very rough shape. If that were the case, would the disciples have developed the level of conviction they had in a risen Jesus?

I would also like to take a minute here to address the claims made in the Quran, since it is somewhat related to this theory. Remember the Quran records that someone else who looked like Jesus died in his place (Qur'an 4:157). Therefore, Jesus never died and later appeared to the disciples as a healthy living person. I looked for any evidence that would support the claim and found literally no historical evidence to support it. The claim would certainly run contrary to the finding of 90 percent of New Testament historians and scholars who consider Jesus' death on the cross to be a historical fact. The other fact this theory would fail to explain is that the tomb the crucified body was buried in was later found empty.[75]

Another theory proposed to explain the empty tomb is that the body of Jesus was stolen as part of a conspiracy undertaken by the followers of Jesus. The Gospel of Matthew records that after hearing that the tomb had been found empty, Jewish authorities spread reports that the body of Jesus was stolen, despite there being Roman guards posted at the tomb entrance (Matthew 27:62–66; 28:11–15). This theory is most strongly refuted by the fact that Jesus' followers sincerely believed they saw him alive again after his death. We know that their behavior and conviction drastically changed following what they sincerely believed to be appearances of the resurrected Jesus. If they had indeed stolen the body, it would not account for this extreme transformation, which is itself considered a historically reliable fact.[76]

A theory often offered to explain the fact that the disciples sincerely believed they saw Jesus alive again after his death is the hallucination theory. Some claim that those undergoing traumatic stress, particularly after the death of a loved one, will experience visions of the deceased person. The problem with this theory is that there are reports that Jesus appeared to *groups* of people after his death. The Gospels report that Jesus appeared to the disciples as a group, and Paul records that Jesus appeared to a group as large as 500 people. Hallucinations are known to be personal events which occur within the mind of the person experiencing them—making it highly unlikely, if not impossible, that more than one person could have experienced the same hallucination.[77]

There are other theories presented in an attempt to explain the historical minimal facts, but there is just one more I would like to address here. Many non-Christian scholars and historians simply contend that any theory proposed to explain the minimal facts presents a more reasonable and logical conclusion than the theory that Jesus was resurrected from the dead. Like scientists, secular scholars and historians argue that supernatural explanations lie beyond the purview and scope of their discipline.[78] While they acknowledge that there is some uncertainty in terms of explaining the minimal facts they do not believe it is logical or reasonable to conclude that Jesus supernaturally rose from the dead. They assume there has to be some other reasonable and logical explanation.

My Decision

Based on the evidence I have studied, I find that the following facts are historically reliable: Jesus died on a cross, the tomb Jesus had been buried in was found empty, Jesus' disciples and previous skeptics sincerely believed they saw Jesus alive again after his death, and there existed a very early Christian creed recording these facts. While this list of facts feels implausibly short, I find them compelling and sufficient, based on strong historical evidence and scholarly acceptance, to reasonably and logically conclude that Jesus of Nazareth was resurrected to life again after being dead.

I realize the enormity of what this statement implies, so let me explain. I will be the first to admit that this conclusion goes against everything we know to be true about our natural world. People do not die and come back to life. We all know that is impossible, according to the natural laws that govern our universe. Resurrection from the dead is one of those things squarely falling into the category of the supernatural. As we know, the study of science and the study of history will not include any notion of the supernatural as a reasonable or logical explanation for anything that happens in our natural world. I very much get their point.

As we have discussed before, it is extremely important that we do not automatically categorize everything we don't understand as "supernatural." If we did that, we would have a very limited understanding of the world around us. However, as I have expressed before, I have concerns that the pendulum is perhaps now swinging too far to the other side of this debate. By requiring *everything* we experience to have a natural explanation, do we continue to limit our understanding of the world around us? At some point, is it justifiable and reasonable to consider evidence that suggests there is something more than natural explanations?

Please don't get me wrong. I am not trying to make this my own personal political statement for the existence of God or his identity. All I am saying is that I personally believe topics such as these can and should be discussed in academic and scholarly venues such as science and history as alternative theories. Like any other theory presented in an academic setting they must meet established guidelines and criteria. If the evidence does not support them as viable, logical, or reasonable theories then so be it. All I am saying is that at the very least, allow the discussion without summarily dismissing them as unscientific, unhistorical, or illogical.

Jumping off the soapbox now and getting back to the issue at hand: To be very honest, I am struggling both emotionally and logically to defend my conclusion that Jesus was resurrected to life again after dying.

Clearly that conclusion necessarily brings with it supernatural elements. I acknowledge that my conclusion on the existence of an intelligent designer also had a supernatural element, but that felt somehow different. That decision placed the intelligent designer outside the boundaries of our universe, which perhaps gave it more legitimacy. Now we are talking about something that occurred within the boundaries of our universe, which makes it feel somehow mystical or paranormal. I cannot reach this conclusion lightly, without much thought, study, and consideration.

I have been thinking about how I would react if someone presented me with a similar mystical or paranormal claim. For example, let's say that someone I respect and historically find to be very reliable tells me that in 2010 someone they know walked to the moon and back. I would probably laugh a little and say, "That's impossible, according to the natural laws that govern our universe, plus—that is just plain ridiculous!" She then responds back to me, "Well, so is the claim that Jesus rose from the dead." I could only respond, "Touché, my friend." However, after processing it for just a minute I would ask, what evidence is there to support the claim? Was the moon-walk event reported to the media after it happened? Were there any eyewitnesses? Does the moonwalker have any souvenirs of his trip, perhaps a moon rock that can be tested for authenticity? Finally, I would ask if Mr. Moonwalker was willing to face persecution and even death to defend his claim? My guess is that the answer to all those questions would be no, presenting absolutely no evidence to support the claim.

The case for the resurrection of Jesus is different. We have the opportunity to assess the claims according to well-established historical methodologies. While we know that historical methodologies cannot prove with certainty what happened in the past, they do provide us a way to assess the historicity and reliability of the claims. These same methodologies apply to all accounts of history. If we were to discredit them, we would have to disregard what we know about the lives and teachings of nearly every historical figure from Socrates to George Washington.

I started my journey to find true north, committed to finding evidence to help me reach well-reasoned, well-supported, logical conclusions about the existence and identity of God. Based on years of study and research, to the best of my ability and due diligence, I find there is evidence to conclude that there is at the very least an intelligent DNA-designer at work in our universe. I now find, based on years of study and research, that there is historical evidence to support the Christian claim that Jesus of Nazareth died on a Roman cross, defied death, and returned to physical life. The only being or force capable of that is one who has power and control over the natural forces of this universe: God.

At this stage, I would like to make it very clear that the conclusions I have reached so far in no way convince me that the "Christian religion" holds all the answers to life or even provides an accurate definition of who God is. I am only saying I believe the evidence supports the claim that Jesus died and resurrected from the dead and that only God would have the power to do that.

Again, you will ultimately have to make a decision for yourself on this issue. As for me, my conclusions now have me asking more questions. If there is historical evidence that the Christian claim is correct and Jesus was God, who came to Earth, what message did he bring? If God came to Earth, he must have had something pretty important to say! I want to know the message Jesus brought to Earth.

PART IV

THE MESSAGE OF GOD

Chapter 11

THE OLD TESTAMENT

The Bible presents us with an opportunity to explore God's message to humanity. This does present some concern, since we have already determined that not every detail of the Bible is likely 100% accurate. For that reason, I do not plan to focus on the specific details of the text, but rather to study and understand its overall message. I also do not intend to study its message in terms of any particular religious viewpoint. I am definitely not interested in someone else's interpretation of how specific verses should dictate the meaningless repetition of various rituals and traditions. What I do intend to do is to study and understand the Bible's message based on what the Bible actually says.

Despite going to Catholic schools all those years, I had never actually read the Bible and, to be honest, knew very little about it. Now excited to learn, I set out energetically and enthusiastically to read the Bible. I am embarrassed to say this, but every time I attempted to read it, I caught myself dozing off. When I was able to push myself to stay awake, I found it all so confusing and could not make sense of it anyway. Despite my best intentions, I was not getting any closer to gaining a meaningful understanding of the Bible. I needed to find another way to go about it.

As I began to explore my options, I discovered many different Bible study resources. They offered insights into the historical context of the time, as well as studied the original languages of the text in Hebrew, Greek and Aramaic. It turns out that studying the original language adds a great deal of context and clarity to the English translations. The other thing these resources helped me do was to make connections between themes, which eventually helped me form what I now find to be a very cohesive, consistent, understandable, and logical Bible message.

I would like to share my research findings on the message of the Bible with you. I am sure you know the drill by now! *Caveat*: I cannot possibly include a full and complete overview of the Bible message, but will do my best to succinctly and accurately summarize what I found. In order to avoid too much distraction from our discussion, I will not be including citations for every single verse or story I reference, but will include some in case you would like to read more on our own. With that, let's roll!

The Old Testament

The word "testament" actually means covenant, agreement, or promise. The Old Testament is essentially a collection of writings explaining God's covenants—in other words, God's agreements and promises to mankind. In case you are not familiar with the Old Testament, let me give you a little more information. As we learned earlier, the Christian Old Testament and the Jewish Hebrew Bible are essentially the same; however, they are arranged a little differently. The Old Testament is a collection of thirty-nine books written by about twenty-three different authors over the course of about 1,500 years.

According to Jewish tradition, the first five books of the Bible were written by Moses sometime around 1400 BCE. These books in the Hebrew Bible are called the Pentateuch. It contains the stories of creation, Adam and Eve, Noah, Abraham, Isaac, Jacob, Joseph, and others who are commonly referred to as the Jewish patriarchs or fathers.

Clearly, Moses was not alive when these earlier events took place. The obvious question is, how could Moses write about these events when he was not there to witness them? It is believed that Moses relied on two things. First, he likely used information preserved in oral traditions that had been passed down from generation to generation. As we know, oral tradition was common during times of antiquity and often served as the only method for transmitting history. Second, many also believe that God divinely inspired Moses with the knowledge he needed to complete the books.

So, why should we care about what this very old and seemingly irrelevant collection of books has to say? I can give you my opinion. After studying it, I feel it helps lay the foundation for God's relationship to his creation, and specifically to people. I am going to give you my best effort summary of the Old Testament. I would encourage you to read it for yourself, or at the very least complete a good Bible study on the Old Testament for a more complete understanding of its message.

The first book of the Old Testament is called Genesis and its very first words are this: "In the beginning God created the heavens and the earth" (Genesis 1:1). It goes on to explain how the earth was formless and that darkness covered the earth. It then explains how God adds light to the day to separate it from the night, how he separates the sky from the earth and the water from land. He then causes the land to produce vegetation, and creates creatures of the sea, birds of the sky, and animals on the land. God looks at his creation and calls it very good.

I would like to stop here to give you a quick example of how attempts to analyze and interpret every word and every last detail of the Bible can go off the rails quickly. Earlier we saw that there is a group of very conservative Christians who believe the Genesis narrative literally describes the way in which God created the universe in six days. Others argue this narrative is representative of how God created the universe. This one debate has caused an extreme amount of dissention not only within the Christian faith but within society as a whole. I would argue it is one of the primary reasons for the extreme divide between science and any notion of God. All I can say is: Who cares if it was a six-day process or six-billion-year process? What would it change? Enough said about that.

God's final and very cherished creation he called man. God said, "Let us make mankind in our image, in our likeness, so that they may rule over the fish of the sea and the birds in the sky, over the livestock and all the wild animals, and over all creatures that move along the ground" (Genesis 1:26). He named the man Adam and created a partner for man, which he called woman and named her Eve. The Genesis account says that God placed Adam and Eve in a beautiful, peaceful garden, which we know as Eden. There they could live in relationship with God and care for his creation. Genesis says that God looked at his creation and called it very good.

I would like to talk for a minute about what it meant when God gave Adam and Eve the responsibility to "rule over" his creation. Some versions of the Bible use the word "dominion" to describe the duty that God gave to Adam and Eve. Most of us who live in the United States probably don't have a very good understanding of the concept of dominion, but those who live in the United Kingdom or one of its colonies likely have a much better understanding. A colony is a country or territory under the political control, or dominion, of a ruling county. Some of you may be familiar with a series of small islands in the Caribbean Sea just southwest of Cuba called the Cayman Islands. The islands are technically under the sovereign control of England and the British crown. England appoints a governor to the region who serves as representative of the ruling country. The role of the governor is to run the islands as if it were part of the United Kingdom. The colony essentially becomes an extension of the ruling country and subject to their control. As a result, the colony is generally protected by the ruling state and is provided assistance during any time of need.[79]

The Bible presents God as establishing earth as a colony of heaven and appointing Adam and Eve as its governors. As governors, Adam and Eve were to have dominion over the earth, to help establish the kingdom of heaven on earth and to multiply. While Adam and Eve had dominion over God's creation, they did not have ultimate authority over it. Ultimate authority for both heaven and earth belonged to God himself (Matthew 28:18). God created rules that Adam and Eve were to follow in order to effectively and successfully rule over his creation. God told Adam and Eve, "You are free to eat from any tree in the garden; but you must not eat from the tree of knowledge of good and evil, for when you eat from it you will certainly die" (Genesis 2:16–17). God had made it clear that in order for Adam and Eve to have dominion over the earth they needed to follow the rules; if they didn't, there would be consequences. Seems fairly straightforward to me—but as you probably already know, this is where the story takes an interesting twist.

It turns out that Adam and Eve were not the only characters in the garden. There was also a dude named Lucifer, better known today as Satan, aka the devil. While we don't know much about Lucifer, there are several verses in the Bible believed to figuratively portray his story. It appears that this guy Lucifer began his career as an archangel in heaven. An archangel is not just your average angel, but one of the highest-ranking angels in heaven. The Bible describes Lucifer as a "perfect angel," full of wisdom and brilliant beauty. Because Lucifer thought very highly of himself, he began a personal campaign in heaven, encouraging other angels to worship and glorify him just as they worshiped and glorified God. In doing so, Lucifer broke one of God's simplest and most important laws: he chose his own self-interests over God's divine will. Because of Lucifer's pride and jealousy, God expelled him from heaven, cast him down to earth, and sentenced him to ultimately die in the fires of hell (Isaiah 14:12–15; Ezekiel 28:12–15; Luke 10:18).

From that time forward the devil made it his number-one mission to turn people away from God, and his first victims were Adam and Eve. Genesis tells us that the devil approached Eve and badmouthed God. He convinced her that God was trying to hide something from her and that eating the fruit of the tree would make her knowledgeable like God. What the devil failed to tell her is that this knowledge would also lead to suffering and death. Unfortunately, Eve takes the devil's bait, eats the fruit, and in turn convinces Adam to eat the fruit as well. God called their disobedience sin. Because of their sin they were forced to leave the garden and live the remainder of their lives on earth separated from God. That separation from God would ultimately result in death. Turns out that little debacle in the garden set off a really bad chain of events in human history.

Since Adam and Eve had legal dominion and power over God's earthly creation, their disobedience essentially resulted in a form of treason. Treason is disloyalty to one's country or government with the intent to overthrow the ruling authority and give it to another. By disobeying God, Adam and Eve relinquished their authority and dominion over the earth to the devil. Satan then essentially became "the ruler of this world" (John 12:31). To this day, Satan continues to use deceit and lies to get people to follow him instead of God. He manipulates people into believing that self-pride and self-glory are better than reliance on God. No wonder there is a lot of bad and evil in this world. Satan relishes in taking as many people down with him as possible.

While the devil may have taken temporary dominion over the earth, he did not win the war. God warns Satan that he has a plan to reclaim his creation and defeat him (Genesis 3:15). The remainder of the Old Testament is the story of how God created a plan to restore his kingdom on earth and rescue his creation from Satan's destruction.

I would like to take another minute to talk about something else that God gave to Adam and Eve as governors of the earth. God gave them the gift of free will—essentially, the ability to choose. Unlike animals which operate on instinct and computers that are programmed, we as human beings have the ability to choose. When you think about it, the ability to choose is a really big deal! If we did not have the freedom of choice, we would be very limited as individuals. We would lose the gift of creativity, personality, our sense of adventure, and many other things that make us unique. Free will, at least in my mind, may be one of the greatest gifts that God gave to mankind. While free will is an awesome gift, it has come with a price: it gives us the ability to choose the *wrong* thing. The culmination of all those wrong choices has resulted in the state of our world today.[80]

God had intended to provide Adam and Eve a perfect place to live as they ruled over the earth. He intended to live in direct relationship with them. While they would work hard serving as governors over the earth, God would make sure that life for them was easy. When Adam and Eve were forced to leave the garden life became hard for them, as well as their descendants, many of whom became important Jewish leaders, as recorded in the book of Genesis. One of the most important was Abraham, who we learned earlier is considered the father of the Jewish religion. God approached Abraham with a plan. He asked Abraham to help reestablish God's kingdom on earth which had been lost to Satan. God told Abraham, that he would become the father of a great nation if he obeyed and respected God. Abraham's descendants became known as the Jewish people and the nation of Israel.

Abraham's son Isaac, Isaac's son Jacob, and Jacob's son Joseph all played important roles in forming the Jewish faith and traditions. During the life of Joseph, many Jews ended up finding refuge in Egypt to escape a great drought in the land of Israel. Jews lived in Egypt for many generations, up until the time of Moses. I would like to spend a little time talking about Moses, as events during his life will be very relevant later on when we talk about Jesus.

The story of Moses begins in the book of Exodus around 1500 BCE. By this time in history the Jewish people had been forced into slavery in Egypt. Like his ancestors before him, God reached out to Moses and asked him to undertake a great task: to lead the Jewish people out of Egypt and back to the land of Israel that God had promised to Abraham. Moses approached the great Pharaoh and ruler of Egypt and demanded that the Jewish people be set free, but the Pharaoh refused.

Through Moses, God sent a series of plagues to the land of Egypt in an attempt to get the Pharaoh to comply and set the people of Israel free (Exodus 7–10). Despite the many devastating plagues brought upon the land, Pharaoh refused. That all changed when God released his final plague on Egypt: the death of the firstborn son of every family in Egypt. On the night that eventually became known as the Passover, God instructed the Jewish people to sacrifice a lamb who was without flaw and to spread its blood above their doorways. The blood would inform the angel of death to pass over their homes. Following the devastation that took place the night of the Passover, Pharaoh agreed to free the Jewish people. Moses led them out of Egypt and into the Sinai desert to begin their journey back to the Promised Land. Remember this story, as we will refer back to it a little later.

It took forty years for Moses and the Jewish people to get back to the land of Israel. Because the journey was long and difficult, the Jewish people became very frustrated and angry with God. Eventually they resorted to worshiping idols and praying to false gods for help. Acknowledging the people's frustration, God set out to renew the covenant he had originally made with Abraham. God essentially said: if you agree to be my people, I will agree to be your God; and if you obey me fully, I will make you my most favored nation and a kingdom of royal priests (see Exodus 19:5–6). It was during this time that God gave Moses the Ten Commandments, along with other moral, civil, and social laws, so the people of Israel knew what God expected of them. Many of these laws were designed to protect the Jewish people from disease and the influences of evil.

The time following the return of the Jewish people to Israel was known as the time of the judges. During this period the Jewish people frequently rebelled and disobeyed God. The judges, generally speaking, were people inspired by God to encourage the Jewish people to stay on the right path, repent, and change their ways. Despite their warnings, the people of Israel continued to disobey God. As a result, God allowed foreign powers to conquer and occupy their cherished nation.

During this time of foreign occupation, the people of Israel realized what their disobedience had done and once again committed to following the laws God had set out for them. As things began to improve, the people of Israel approached God with a request: they asked God to give them a king to help them reestablish his kingdom of heaven on earth. God granted their request, and a long line of kings reigned over the nation of Israel, the greatest of whom was King David. As in the past, corruption and disobedience caused problems for the Jewish people and they again fell out of favor with God. It was during this time that God sent great prophets to the nation of Israel to deliver messages of warning to the people. They warned that if the people continued to disobey God, there would be consequences.

Among the many prophets who preached repentance and judgment there was one prophet who brought a unique message of hope to the nation of Israel; his name was Isaiah. In his prophesies Isaiah made reference to a coming Messiah who would be born of a virgin (Isaiah 7:14), proclaim good news (Isaiah 61:1), die a sacrificial death (Isaiah 52:13–53:12), and return to claim his people (Isaiah 60:2–3). Isaiah refers to this Messiah as a gentle redeemer who would be rejected by mankind (Isaiah 42:1–4; 53:3) and set captives free (Isaiah 61:1).

As prophets continued to warn the Israelites of the dangers of disobeying God, things went from bad to worse. The northern kingdom of Israel fell to the Assyrians in around 722 BCE. While the southern kingdom of Judah was able to hold the Assyrians off, they too fell to the foreign power of Babylon around 587 BCE. Much of the Jewish population was relocated to Babylon and remained there until about 538 BCE, when they were allowed to return to their homeland. Probably the most notable Jewish figure of this time was a young man named Daniel. You may know the story of Daniel in the lion's den. Because of Daniel's steadfast devotion to the God of Israel, Darius, the pagan king of Media who now ruled Babylon, ordered him to be put to death. His sentence was to be thrown into a den of hungry lions who would devour him. Instead, God protected Daniel and the lions did not harm him; instead, it was Daniel's accusers who were eaten by the lions. Daniel's obedience and love for God served as a great example of what God will do for those who choose to love him.

This marks the end of what are referred to as the Jewish historical books of the Bible describing events of the time. The remaining
books are known as wisdom books, which include books like Psalms and
Proverbs. These books are collections of songs, poems, and words of
wisdom written by various authors. There is also a series of books that
were written by people known as the minor prophets. These prophets
lived at various times throughout the Jewish history just covered. They
too brought messages of both warning, repentance, and the hope of
redemption and restoration.

Between the Old and New Testament

The last book of the Old Testament was Malachi, written in the mid-
400s BCE. At this point, God pretty much went radio-silent. Based on
the messages delivered by the prophets, the Jewish people had great hope
that God would be sending them a great messiah to redeem them. We
know from other historical records that the four hundred years between
the last writings of the Old Testament and the first writings of the New
Testament brought more change for the people of Israel. The events of
this time very much set the political and cultural stage for the New Testament and the world into which Jesus was born. Politically and militarily
the nation of Israel continued to be controlled by various foreign powers. The Persians were in control as the temple and the city of Jerusalem
were rebuilt. Around the year 332 BCE Alexander the Great and his
powerful Macedonian (Greek) army conquered the Persians and took
control of Israel.

The Greek influence on the region was profound. The Greeks
brought their language, culture, architecture, and government to the
nation of Israel. The Greek (Seleucid) occupation of the region eventually caused some hardship for the Jewish people. Some of the Greek
factions were brutal and even forced the Jews to practice pagan religions
or be killed. It was this series of events that led to what was known as
the Maccabean Revolt against the Greeks. Hanukkah is the celebration

of the Jewish victory over Greek oppression, which Jews continue to celebrate to this day.

During this time Israel experienced a brief time of independence. It was also during this time that two main Jewish religious groups emerged. The Pharisees were a group that supported strict observance of Jewish traditions and laws. They believed that if the Jewish people were legally bound to follow religious laws, God would protect the nation from continued foreign oppression and hardship. Leaders within the Pharisee sect were called rabbis. The other Jewish sect at this time was the Sadducees, who believed that the nation could actually benefit from foreign powers in terms of education and other societal benefits. Leaders of the Sadducee sect were referred to as priests. The two groups had differing views on how to follow and interpret the Torah law, which on occasion created conflict.

In about the year 63 BCE the Roman Empire took control of Jerusalem and the nation of Israel. While under the political control of the Romans, Judaism was recognized as the legal religion of the region. The Romans allowed local leaders to serve in the Roman government set up in their home territories. After serving in several different capacities for the Romans, a man of Jewish descent by the name of Herod (also known as Herod the Great) was bestowed the title of King of Judea by the Roman Senate. Although Herod was often referred to as "King of the Jews" he was not admired by the Jewish people. He served as king over the nation of Israel until his death in 4 BCE. During that time, Herod led many celebrated architectural projects, including the renovation of the second Jewish temple into a massive and impressive architectural structure. Following his death in 4 BCE, his kingdom was divided between his four sons. His sons were also known as oppressive rulers. Herod's son Archelaus was so destructive that the Roman leadership removed him from power in Jerusalem and replaced him with a Roman governor named Pontius Pilate.

This is where the New Testament picks up the story. Remember, the New Testament writings are from a Christian perspective, so they are no longer considered Jewish writings or scripture. As we have seen, the Old Testament is a compilation of Jewish history, worship books, and prophecies. It covers the story of creation, God's process of identifying the Jews as his chosen people, and the cycle of oppression and restoration they endured. In my opinion the main message of the Old Testament is that the people of God prosper when they follow his laws and suffer greatly when they turn away from him and follow their own agenda. Despite their continued disobedience, God made a promise to send the Jewish people a messiah who would restore their status as God's chosen nation. Many Jews believed that the coming messiah would be a military ruler who would regain control of the land through military force. Understanding that historical context is critical to understanding the story of Jesus of Nazareth, which we will now look at in the New Testament.

Chapter 12

THE NEW TESTAMENT

Let's start by looking at a few of the New Testament logistics. The New Testament is made up of twenty-seven books. As we learned earlier, the word "testament" means covenant. The New Testament tells us about the new covenant (promise) that God makes with his people on earth through Jesus. As we have seen, the first four books of the New Testament are called Gospels. The Gospels are focused on documenting the life, death, and resurrection of Jesus. Following the four Gospels is a book called the Acts of the Apostles which was written by Luke, the same author as the gospel, followed by several epistles (letters) by Jesus' disciples. These writings tell us about events that took place in the early church and provide us deeper insight into the message of Jesus. The final book of the New Testament is the book of Revelation, written by the same author as the Gospel of John describing the second coming of Jesus.

As always, I have a caveat. Because there is a lot going on in the Gospels, we will only have time to explore Jesus' message at a high level. I would very much encourage you to take the time at some point to read the New Testament for yourself for more detail. My primary goal will be to provide a brief overview of the gospel narratives, specifically focused on the message of Jesus. I am hopeful that it will serve as a good foundation so that you can develop a better understanding of who Jesus was, the message he delivered, and how that message applies to your life. Again, in order to avoid too much distraction from our discussion I will not include citations for every single verse or message I refer to. I will include some, in case you would like to read more on your own.

By the way, the word "gospel" means "good news." Even more specifically, it means good news in the sense of a big public announcement like "breaking news." Let's see what the big news is!

Overview of the Gospel Narratives

The Gospels of Luke and Matthew begin by telling us a little bit about the birth narrative surrounding Jesus. Matthew provides some detail about the birth of Jesus, but beyond that there is not much documenting the childhood of Jesus. All four of the Gospels mainly focus on the public ministry of Jesus, which started when he was about thirty years old. Jesus' public ministry began when he was baptized by a man named John the Baptist. John the Baptist lived a very simple life, living off the land in the wilderness area northeast of Jerusalem near the Jordan River. There he spent his time boldly teaching and preaching that the Messiah prophesied in the Jewish scriptures was coming soon. He told people to repent—to have a change of heart and mind—in preparation for the Messiah's coming. As people committed to repenting and changing their ways, John baptized them in the Jordan River. Baptism symbolized their desire to wash away past sins and to move forward as new people committed to living within God's will. People traveled from all around to hear John's message and to be baptized.

One day as John was teaching, he noticed a man off in the distance. As that man approached, John proclaimed to those around him, "Look, the lamb of God, who takes away the sin of the world!" (John 1:29). That man was Jesus. Take note of how John referenced Jesus as the "Lamb of God"; we will talk more about this a little later.

When Jesus reached the river, he asked John to baptize him. As John baptized Jesus, it is recorded that the sky opened and the Spirit of the Lord landed on Jesus in the form of a dove. A voice from above proclaimed, "This is my Son, whom I love; with him I am well pleased" (Matthew 3:16–17). Another important thing to note about this narrative is that God revealed himself in three different ways. He spoke as God the Father about Jesus, who is God the Son, on whom God the Spirit came to rest. This concept of God as three separate individuals became known as the Trinity.

The Gospels of Matthew, Mark, and Luke record that following his baptism, Jesus went out into the desert wilderness alone for forty days. During that time, he fasted and prayed. It was also reported that on several occasions Satan visited Jesus and taunted him. Satan tempted Jesus with his worldly power; remember, Satan gained that power as a result of usurping dominion over the earth from Adam and Eve. Satan told Jesus, "All this I will give you . . . if you will bow down and worship me" (Matthew 4:9). Each time, Jesus rebuked Satan. The Gospels record that Jesus relied on God the Father and the Spirit who was with him to give him the strength and perseverance he needed to get through that time of trial.

After his time in the wilderness, Jesus emerged ready to begin his public ministry. One of the very first messages Jesus taught was, "Repent, for the kingdom of heaven (God) is near." (Matthew 4:17). The Gospels record that Jesus began traveling from town to town, teaching about the kingdom of God and performing great miracles. Jesus declared that this was the reason he was sent (Luke 4:43).

As his popularity with the people continued to grow, Jesus' message became even bolder. While teaching in a synagogue in his hometown of Nazareth, the Gospel of Luke records that Jesus was reading a passage from the Old Testament book of Isaiah. The passage he was reading was known to contain a description of the prophesied Messiah. Jesus read from the ancient scripture, "The Spirit of the Lord is upon me, because he has anointed me to proclaim good news to the poor. He has sent me to proclaim freedom for the prisoners and the recovery of sight for the blind, to set the oppressed free, to proclaim the year of the Lord's favor." Jesus then said to the crowd around him, "Today this Scripture has been fulfilled in your hearing" (Luke 4:18–19). Whoa! Was Jesus actually claiming to be the prophesied Jewish Messiah? People were shocked as the statement began to sink in. Eventually emotions began to escalate and people were outraged by the claim he had just made. The crowd attempted to lead Jesus to a cliff, where they intended to push him over. Jesus simply walked away, commenting that no prophet is ever accepted in their hometown.

During the early stages of his ministry, Jesus selected a group of twelve men to travel with him and to help him spread his kingdom message. These men became known as Jesus' disciples. During this time Jesus taught primarily in a region of Israel called Galilee, which is the area around the Sea of Galilee. Soon, news about Jesus spread and people came from miles around to hear him teach about the kingdom of God and to seek his healing. The Gospels record that people were amazed by Jesus' teachings, the authority with which he spoke, and the healings he was able to perform.

Curious, people began to ask Jesus more about the kingdom he taught about. The answer Jesus provided became one of his best-known teachings which today we call the Sermon on the Mount. Jesus taught that the kingdom of God was very different than the kingdom of the world. While the world defines success as power and wealth, Jesus taught that in the kingdom of God success is defined by sacrifice and service to others. Jesus provided a list of these attributes and the blessings they provide. Today we refer to this list of blessings as the Beatitudes.[81]

During the Sermon on the Mount Jesus also refers to the laws of the kingdom and teaches people how to pray. He instructed people to pray to God as if he was their father. Jesus used the Aramaic word *Abba* to describe God. In English that word is translated as "daddy," inferring a close personal relationship between God and people. He also instructed them to pray that the will of God be done on the kingdom of earth just as it is in the kingdom of heaven. We will go into a little more detail on the message Jesus delivered in the Sermon on the Mount later, but I highly recommend you read it on your own as well. It provides great instruction on the culture of God's kingdom and how we can live according to God's will (Matthew 5:1–7:28; Luke 6:20–49).

By now, you are probably picking up on the fact that Jesus' message very much focused on the kingdom of God. During one of Jesus' visits to the capital city of Jerusalem, a Jewish religious leader by the name of Nicodemus came to visit Jesus in the middle of the night so as not to attract attention. Nicodemus acknowledged that Jesus must have been sent by God, as evidenced by his great signs and miracles, but he wanted to know more about the kingdom Jesus taught about. Nicodemus asked Jesus how one can enter the kingdom of God. Jesus told him that no one could enter the kingdom of God unless they were "born again." Nicodemus was confused, wondering how it was possible for anyone to be *physically* born again. Jesus explained that to be born again meant a *spiritual* death—to die to your old way of life focused on worldly things, and to begin a new life guided by the Spirit of God.

It was during this conversation that Jesus made a very important statement about the purpose for which he was sent: "For God so loved the world, that he gave his only Son, that whoever believes in him should not perish but have eternal life. For God did not send his Son into the world to condemn the world, but in order that the world might be saved through him" (John 3:16–17). In this statement Jesus highlights the two main reasons he came to Earth: to bring salvation to those who love him and to reestablish the kingdom of God.

The Gospels are filled with many more stories of Jesus' travels and the miracles he performed. It is recorded that Jesus healed many people suffering from both physical and mental illnesses. It is also recorded that Jesus exhibited great power over the forces of nature, such as the ability to calm storms and to walk on water. The Gospels record that large crowds of people began to follow him, learning from him and seeking his healing. Later in his ministry Jesus was not only gaining public attention, but was gaining political attention as well. Remember that during this time in history the Romans held political power in Israel, but the Jewish religious leaders had a great deal of authority on religious matters. Jesus' teachings often challenged the teachings and authority of the Jewish religious leaders. Jesus called them "hypocrites," as they often imposed harsh legal restrictions on the Jewish people but found excuses to exempt themselves from those same requirements. Jesus very boldly denounced hypocrisy.

One day while teaching in the temple in Jerusalem Jesus taught, "Beware of the teachers of the law. They like to walk around in flowing robes and love to be greeted with respect in the marketplaces and have the most important seats in the synagogues and the places of honor at banquets. They devour widows' houses and for a show make lengthy prayers. These men will be punished most severely" (Luke 20:46). The Jewish leaders knew Jesus was talking about them and took great offense. As they became more disgruntled with the teachings of Jesus, you might say they began to stalk him. They wanted to keep tabs on what this Jesus guy was doing and saying.

Jesus continued to make bold claims as he preached. One day as he was healing a paralytic man, he told the man that his sins were forgiven. Upon hearing this, the religious leaders who had followed him became outraged. Everyone knew that only God could forgive sins! Who did this dude Jesus think he was—God? Jesus further angered religious leaders by healing people on the Sabbath day. According to Jewish law, no work, not even healings, were to be conducted on the Sabbath day. Jewish leaders witnessing the event confronted Jesus about his clear violation of Jewish law. Jesus responded to them by saying, "My Father is working even now, so I am working" (John 5:17). Was Jesus now claiming he was the Son of God? Jewish leaders began to discuss a plan for dealing with this lying troublemaker named Jesus.

As things continued to heat up, Jesus decided to back off a little. He began to teach in what are known as parables. Parables are stories designed to illustrate a moral or spiritual lesson through analogy. Jesus taught in parables to avoid further unwanted attention from the religious leaders. He was still able to teach valuable lessons about the kingdom, but the messages were hidden in simple stories that were less likely to be politically charged. We will take a look at some of these parables in more detail a little later.

As the disciples spent more and more time with Jesus, they began to gain some clarity about who he actually was. One day while traveling in the northern part of Israel Jesus asked his disciples, "Who do you say I am?" Peter, who had taken on a leadership role amongst the disciples, said, "You are the Messiah, the Son of the living God" (Matthew 16:15–16). As Jesus' message began to sink in and solidify in the hearts and minds of his followers, he shared another important message with them—about his impending death.

I would like to take some time to talk about the events that led up to the death of Jesus on the cross. We know from our previous study that it is a historically reliable fact that Jesus of Nazareth was killed on a Roman cross. It is important to understand the historical events that led up to such a cruel and harsh death.

Jesus and his disciples were traveling to Jerusalem to celebrate the Passover. Remember that Passover commemorated the night the angel of death passed over the homes of the Jews enslaved in Egypt. As Jesus and his disciples approached the city, large groups of people began to follow them. Many began to proclaim that Jesus was in fact the Jewish messiah that they had been waiting for. They cheered and threw palm branches on the ground in front of him, calling him "King of the Jews" as he entered the city gates riding on a donkey. Today, many commemorate this event on the Sunday before Easter, and refer to it as Palm Sunday.

The ironic thing about this royal procession into the city was that the Jewish people had always believed that the prophesied messiah would be a great military leader—that he would free them from foreign control and make them a great and powerful nation. The person they were now hailing as Messiah taught a message of peace and love and rode on a donkey! What great military leader rides on a donkey? As you can imagine, this whole event caught the attention of the Jewish leaders who had also gathered in the city for Passover. You might say it was the straw that finally broke the camel's back. Now people were idolizing the guy as the Jewish Messiah. They'd had enough of this guy who was misrepresenting himself and had the nerve to claim to be the Son of God.

The Gospels present other detailed events that occurred during the week of Passover. For the sake of time, we will focus on the arrest and subsequent trial of Jesus. The Jewish leaders eventually had Jesus arrested and charged him with the crime of blasphemy. Blasphemy was the act of insulting God, which under Jewish law was a capital offense. This brings up a very important point. There are people who argue that Jesus never actually claimed to be God. They present this argument to suggest that Jesus' divinity was an exaggeration added to the story years after his death and therefore legend, not historical fact. It is accurate to say that the Bible never presents Jesus as running around proclaiming, "I am God, I am God!" However, it is clear that throughout his public ministry Jesus proclaims his divinity in much more subtle ways.

It was not until standing trial for blasphemy that Jesus made the boldest claim of his divinity. During the trial, the high priest Caiaphas asked Jesus point blank, "Are you the Christ, the Son of the Blessed one?" Jesus answered, "I am." (Mark 14:61–62). At that point the chief priest tore his clothes and immediately declared him guilty. If anyone ever presents you with the argument that Jesus never claimed to be God, ask them this simple question. "Then why did they kill him?" The answer is: Jesus was sentenced to death for the crime of blasphemy because he claimed to be God.

Since the Jewish religious leaders did not have the political authority to execute Jesus for his crimes, they took him to the Roman political authorities and requested that *they* put Jesus to death. They convinced the Roman authorities that Jesus' claim to be "King of the Jews" was an attempt to overthrow the Roman government. That amounted to an act of treason and was punishable by death under Roman law. While Roman authorities did not find a strong case against him, Jewish leaders insisted that Jesus be put to death. Thus, Jesus was brutally flogged by the Romans and nailed to a cross, where he died.

After his death it is recorded that a man named Joseph of Arimathea, who was himself a Jewish religious leader, offered his own tomb in which to bury Jesus. We know from our earlier study that when the women followers of Jesus went to the tomb three days later to anoint his body with spices, they discovered the tomb was empty. Today Christians commemorate this as Easter.

It is recorded that Jesus appeared to his disciples several times during the forty-day period following his death. During that time Jesus continued to teach them about the kingdom of God and instructed them about how they would receive the Holy Spirit after he left. On the fortieth day Jesus was taken up to heaven from the Mount of Olives, where the book of Revelation says he will return again to physically reclaim his kingdom. As Jesus was leaving the earth he said to his disciples, "All authority in heaven and on earth has been given to me. Therefore, go and make disciples of all nations, baptizing them in the name of the Father and of the Son and of the Holy Spirit, and teaching them to obey everything I have commanded you. And surely I am with you always, to the very end of the age" (Matthew 28:16).

Ten days later, on the day known as Pentecost, the Holy Spirit came to the disciples who were gathered together in a room. It is recorded that a wind filled the room and there appeared to be flames above their heads. From that point forward the disciples, who were once full of fear, went out and boldly proclaimed the message of Jesus. As we saw from our earlier studies, the fact that the disciples sincerely believed they saw Jesus alive again after his death is a historically reliable fact accepted by the far majority of historians and scholars.

Chapter 13

WHAT DOES IT ALL MEAN?

Now that we have completed a high-level overview and have some context around the ministry of Jesus, I would like to take some time to try and gain a better understanding of what his message actually means. I guess you could call it a mini-Bible study. The purpose of a Bible study is to consider the historical context, the meaning of the original language, and the bigger picture in order to understand the comprehensive and deeper message of Jesus.

Growing up I was taught that the reason Jesus came to Earth was to save us from our sins—that Jesus took the wrath of an angry God in our place so that all we had to do was to believe in Jesus and we would be saved. What confused me was the fact that there were all these other rules that, if broken, seemed to somehow put that salvation at risk. Eventually I realized there was no way I could keep all those rules, which left me feeling very lost when life started falling apart around me.

I have come to realize that much of what I once considered to be my "faith" was in reality a combination of worldly elements that pulled me in the direction of *magnetic* north. I have come to realize that what I was taught to be the exclusive message of Jesus was only part of the story. As I read and studied the Gospels for myself, it was very apparent that I had missed a very significant part of Jesus' message. The words "kingdom of God" literally jumped out at me over and over again as I made my way through the Gospels. While I had certainly heard the concept before, it never seemed particularly relevant to me. What I discovered, through further study, was that it was the most profound and relevant message in the entire Bible.

As I continued to learn more about the significance of the kingdom of God and how it fit in to the overall message of Jesus, things suddenly began to make sense. The Old Testament, Jesus' message, evil and good, death and life, salvation and the kingdom, it all suddenly fit together and created an amazing portrait of God's love and purpose for his creation. I would like to share some of the questions that I asked and the answers I found, in the hope it can help you to get a better understanding of the true meaning of Jesus' message.

What Is the Kingdom of God?

The short answer is that the kingdom of God is his eternal government and authority over his territories, which includes both heaven and earth. Remember back to the story of Genesis when God first established earth as a territorial extension or colony of heaven. God created Adam and Eve in his own image to have dominion over the territory of earth; they were essentially to serve as the colony's governors and to serve as God's representatives to care for and manage earth just like heaven.

Unfortunately, we know how that turned out. God gave Adam and Eve the gift of free will. While that is an amazing gift, if it is used in the wrong ways it becomes a deadly curse. Adam and Eve were derailed by Satan's deception, which resulted in defiance of God's laws—sin. Sin breaks the life-giving connection between God and his human creation. When Adam and Eve sinned, they handed over dominion of the earth to a very corrupt and evil governor.

Does God Have a Plan?

Yes, God's plan to deal with Satan is a two-phased approach, with his commander-in-chief being Jesus.

Phase 1: The first phase was carried out two thousand years ago when Jesus came to Earth. During phase 1 of the plan, Jesus came to accomplish two primary missions.

- First, Jesus came to destroy the power Satan has over death by dying on the cross.

- Second, and equally important, is that Jesus showed us the key to living good and meaningful life here on Earth and gave all of us the opportunity to reclaim our rightful place in the kingdom of God. I will explain more about the significance of this in just a minute.

Phase 2: In phase 2 of God's plan Jesus will return to Earth and physically take dominion of the earth back from Satan and destroy him.

What Did Jesus' Death Accomplish during Phase 1?

I asked you earlier to file a few things away for later discussion. One was the story of the original Passover event, when Moses instructed the Jewish people held in slavery to wipe the blood of a perfect lamb above their doorway. That blood was a sign that the angel of death should pass over that home and spare the lives of those inside. The other thing I asked you to file away was the statement made by John the Baptist when he first saw Jesus. Remember his statement, "Behold the lamb of God who takes away the sins of the world." It turns out there is a very strong correlation between these two events and the death of Jesus on the cross.

To help me better understand exactly what Jesus accomplished by dying on the cross I imagine this scenario: When Lucifer (Satan) turned against God in heaven, God kicked him out of heaven and banished him to earth. Because of his disobedience Satan was marked for eternal separation from God and ultimately death. Because God requires perfect justice, anyone else who is guilty of the same offense (sin) deserves the same punishment. To spite God, Satan does everything in his power to ensure that God's cherished human creation meets the same fate he did. I picture Satan taking a thick black permanent marker and placing a giant X on each of us when we sin, noting that we too deserve to die for turning against God. The only thing capable of removing the mark of death is the blood of a perfect sacrifice. In the story of Moses and the Israelites, people were saved by the blood of a perfect lamb placed over their doorway. In the story of Jesus, people were saved by the blood of a perfect person. Jesus' blood serves to wash away the mark of death that Satan had placed on us and ultimately signals to the angel of death to pass by us.

How Much Does God Love Us?

A very significant message throughout the entire Bible is God's love for his human creation. That message is easy to miss if you do not understand the significance of the kingdom of God and his overall plan. God did not create us to be his servants or his minions; he created us to be like him, to represent him and to have dominion over his earthly kingdom. When people lost the kingdom, God loved them so much that he created a plan to restore them to their rightful place in his kingdom. Let's look at a few examples.

Of course, the greatest display of God's love for us was when his Son Jesus died on the cross. We have seen from our studies that death on a Roman cross was an excruciatingly painful and humiliating death. Jesus agreed to that death in order to save us from the death we deserved. He offered himself as the perfect sacrifice in order to wash away the mark of death that had been placed on us as the result of our choice to sin. This could arguably be the greatest act of love in all of human history.

Another example of God's love for his people is the parable of the prodigal son. This parable illustrates God's love for us as our father in his kingdom. The story tells of a son who wants to leave his father's home. He requests that his father give him his inheritance so he could move away and do his own thing. Over the course of several years the son foolishly spends his money and is eventually left with nothing. Desperate to find help, but knowing how deeply he hurt his father, he decides to ask if he can return to his father's home as a mere servant, knowing he was no longer worthy of being called his son. As he approached the house, his father immediately recognized him and ran to meet him. He flung his arms around his son and welcomed him back with great love and respect. Not only did he celebrate his son's return but he restored him to his rightful position in the family (Luke 15:11). Jesus says this is how God welcomes us back into the kingdom even after we sin. That sounds like an amazing kind of love.

What Is the Culture of the Kingdom?

Many of Jesus' teachings were designed to illustrate the differences between the kingdom of God and the kingdom of the world. I would like to take a closer look at the Beatitudes, as they serve to describe the unique culture of the kingdom of God. This study is a good example of how looking at the original Aramaic language can help us better understand the English translation.

The original Aramaic word for "beatitude" meant "blessing," but it went even deeper than that. It meant the kind of blessing that brought great happiness and bliss. In other words, Jesus is saying that in the kingdom there are values that, when lived out, bring with them much happiness, success, and blessing. Let's look at them one at a time.

- "Blessed are the poor in spirit, for theirs is the kingdom of heaven" (Matthew 5:3). In the original Aramaic, the words used in the first beatitude meant much more than to be poor in spirit.

It meant to be firmly based, grounded, and focused while being humble, unassuming, and surrendered. Blessed are those who are firmly and humbly grounded in God.

- "Blessed are they who mourn, for they will be comforted" (Matthew 5:4). This would have described someone who struggles with feelings of being lost. Jesus tells us that in the kingdom of God when we are lost, yet desire to find our way home, God will help us and comfort us on the journey back—very different than the worldly culture we experience today, where those suffering from anxiety and depression are often left behind.

- "Blessed are the meek, for they will inherit the earth" (Matthew 5:5). The words used in the original Aramaic included the concepts of gentleness, flexibility, self-awareness, self-control, submission to God, and reliance on his strength. Jesus is telling us that in his kingdom success is achieved by gentleness, self-control, and an awareness of how our behavior affects others.

- "Blessed are they who hunger and thirst for righteousness, for they will be filled" (Matthew 5:6). The words used here would describe someone who intensely craves justice and equality and proactively works to recognize the mutual value of all who live in the kingdom.

- "Blessed are the merciful, for they will be shown mercy" (Matthew 5:7). The Aramaic words not only included the concept of mercy, but also compassion, so much so that compassion and mercy radiate from a person's inner spirit. In the kingdom of God caring and having compassion for others is valued and blessed.

- "Blessed are the pure of heart, for they will see God" (Matthew 5:8). In the original language this included the concepts of sincerity, clarity, consistency, radiating love, and electrifying purpose. In other words, Jesus is saying those who exude love and consistently live with the purpose of loving others are valued in the kingdom of God.

- "Blessed are the peacemakers, for they will be called children of God" (Matthew 5:9). The Aramaic not only referred to making peace but planting peace. These are words of action that would describe someone who intentionally and purposefully plants peace in hope that it will grow and blossom.

- "Blessed are they who are persecuted because of righteousness, for theirs is the kingdom of heaven" (Matthew 5:10). Those who are persecuted for following God and promoting the values of his kingdom will be rewarded in the kingdom.

While the Beatitudes serve as guidelines for behavior, they also describe how the culture within the kingdom of God is very different from the culture of the world. Imagine a society where these values are encouraged, respected, and rewarded. Wouldn't it be awesome to live there?

What Are the Laws of the Kingdom?

An important part of living in a society under the rule of a governmental body is understanding its governing laws. Laws are essentially the standards by which we agree to live by when we are a member of that society. Laws are a necessary part of living together in harmony with each other and with nature. Without laws everyone's individual interests and desires would collide which would result in pure chaos and destruction. Laws are an important part of setting boundaries and expectations, and of ensuring that people can pursue their goals and enjoy life while coexisting with others in fairness and rightness.

In the United States and many other countries these governing laws are referred to as the country's constitution. In a democratic government such as the United States the constitution is created by the consensus of the people and what they want and expect from the government. A kingdom's constitution is different. A kingdom's constitution is established by the sovereign (king and/or queen) and reflects their will for their territory. Obviously, one can see the importance of having a compassionate, loving, and honest king who treats citizens like his children rather than as subjects or slaves.

When God gave Adam and Eve dominion over the earth, he established laws. While they had great discretion regarding how they would run and manage the earth, God told them they were never to eat from the tree of the knowledge of good and evil. When they openly chose to defy that law, they lost their right to have dominion over the earth and to be citizens of the kingdom. At that point they lost all the privileges, rights, and the protections the kingdom provided them. Life got very difficult for Adam and Eve!

Let me share a little scenario I think demonstrates the importance of laws as we live and operate in community with other people and with nature. In my backyard I have a spot I call my serenity garden. I started it years ago when I was in the midst of the challenges of being a single mom raising three teenage girls. The serenity garden gave me a place to find some peace and get some nature therapy while staying close to what was happening at home.

Imagine if the serenity garden suddenly became a wildly popular place and others wanted to contribute to the beauty of the garden. I would be flattered and very much enjoy having help with it. I would, however, have to set some rules. The most important rule would be that no one could bring any type of invasive vegetation into the garden. Even though some of those invasive plants look harmless and can even be kind of pretty, they have the potential to completely take over the garden and kill the other flowers and plants that grow there.

I suspect this is the reason God had to set rules in his garden as well. If he were to let Adam and Eve plant sin and disobedience in the garden, it had the potential to grow and eventually kill what was good and beautiful in the garden. The rules were not established to dominate, control, or place unreasonable or unfair restrictions on them; they were created to show them what they needed to avoid if the garden was to remain good, beautiful, and right.

If we choose to live in the kingdom of God, we too must live according to the law. I think it is very important to remember that God's laws are not meant to restrain, persecute, or punish us; they are meant to instruct us on what we can do to avoid and prevent anguish, pain, unhappiness, and destruction. If we knowingly choose to disobey those laws, we have to know we are risking our own happiness and safety, which will likely also affect the happiness and safety of others around us.

During his ministry Jesus was asked, "Teacher, which is the greatest commandment in the law?" Jesus answered, "Love the Lord your God with all your heart and with all your soul and with all your mind.' This is the first and greatest commandment. And the second is like it: 'Love your neighbor as yourself.' All the Law and the Prophets hang on these two commandments" (Matthew 22:36–40).

While the laws of the kingdom sound very simple, they are far from easy to uphold! Many of Jesus' other teachings describe more specific ways in which we can love God and others in order to accomplish this great commandment.

How Do We Become Citizens of the Kingdom?

We saw earlier that Nicodemus, one of the Jewish religious leaders, asked Jesus this exact question. Jesus said to him, "Very truly I tell you, no one can see the kingdom of God unless they are born again" (John 3:3). Jesus explained that being born again starts with a heart of repentance. Repentance is the act of turning away from our old worldly ways and aligning ourselves with the kingdom culture. Once we very intentionally make that decision to repent, we have to accept the invitation that Jesus extends to us through his death and resurrection. Jesus said, "I am the way the truth and the life. No one comes to the Father except through me" (John 14:6). When we accept that Jesus died for our sins, his blood removes the mark of death. At that point we have been reborn into the kingdom of God.

There are some who believe that baptism is a formal requirement to being "saved." While Jesus does not specifically mention baptism as a requirement for entering the kingdom of God, he seems to encourage it. After all, he himself was baptized. In addition, as he was leaving the earth he instructed his disciples to go and make disciples of all nations and baptize them in the name of the Father, Son, and Holy Spirit. It certainly seems like a great way to outwardly profess one's faith and to make a commitment to Jesus and life within the kingdom of God.

Our Rights as Citizens of the Kingdom of God

As citizens of any country, there are rights and privileges associated with citizenship. When we accept Jesus' invitation to the kingdom, we essentially gain dual citizenship. We remain citizens of our country here on Earth, but we also belong to the kingdom of God where we have rights, privileges, and protection.

Jesus taught, "But seek first the kingdom and his righteousness, and all these things will be given to you as well" (Matthew 6:33). What did Jesus mean by all these things will be given to you when we seek the kingdom first?

Jesus mentions many benefits to kingdom citizenship, but here are a few that particularly jump out at me:

- First and foremost, as citizens of the kingdom the greatest gift we are given is the gift of the Holy Spirit. When Jesus lived on this earth he was guided and strengthened by the Holy Spirit, who enabled him to do amazing and powerful things. Jesus promised his disciples that when he returned to heaven, he would send them the gift of the Holy Spirit (John 14:16). Jesus described the Holy Spirit as someone who would guide them, show them the truth, and give them strength and wisdom. Jesus said that while they would not be able to see the Spirit, like the wind they would hear him and feel the effects of his presence (John 3:8). The Spirit changes us, and as a result we produce the fruits of the Spirit: love, joy, peace, patience, kindness, goodness, faithfulness, gentleness, and self-control (Galatians 3:22–23).

- Jesus also tells us that as citizens of the kingdom, God has granted us forgiveness for our sins, which means we will not face judgment or be condemned but have eternal life in the kingdom to come (John 3:18).

- As citizens of the kingdom, we do not need to worry. This is a really big one for so many of us who live with a ton of anxiety every day. Jesus tells us that he will always provide everything we need (Matthew 6:25).

- We are also told that as citizens of the kingdom to "ask and it will be given to you; seek and you will find; knock and the door will be opened to you" (Luke 11:9). He may not always answer our prayers immediately or the way we want him to, but if we are patient and trust in him, he will provide us with answers and blessings far beyond anything we ever expected.

What Is Our Role in the Kingdom?

When Jesus left the earth, he told his followers (and us) to go and make disciples of all nations and essentially to teach them the ways of the kingdom (Matthew 28:16). This has become known as the Great Commission. In one of Paul's letters to the Corinthians he describes this role like that of an ambassador (2 Corinthians 5:18). We can think of this very much like the role of a political ambassador today. Ambassadors are people from one country who are politically appointed to represent the interests of their nation in another country. Ambassadors are given authority to speak on behalf of their government, but they must uphold the laws, culture, and character of their host nation at all times. Good ambassadors will have strong leadership skills; they will be resilient and well respected.[82]

Our role as citizens of God's kingdom is to be his ambassadors on earth. We are to represent our kingdom's interests, to uphold the laws, and reflect the culture and character of the kingdom of God. In one of his teachings, Jesus pointed out that we are to be what he called "salt" and "light" (Matthew 5:13–16). This is another great example of how studying the historical context of the time can help add meaning and clarity to the gospel message. Salt in the ancient world was an extremely valuable resource. Salt was not only a spice that flavored food, but it was also often added to food as a preservative to hinder the process of decay. When Jesus instructed people to be the "salt of the earth," he meant that they should not only add flavor to the lives of those around them but also preserve what was good in the world and prevent moral decay.

Jesus also teaches that those who live as citizens of the kingdom should serve as a light to the world. The Greek word used for "light" referred to something very bright, like the light that emanates from a lighthouse, safely guiding ships and keeping them from harm. Jesus says that this light represents the light of the Spirit that burns brightly within us. We are to let that light shine on the message of Jesus, to reveal its guiding truth and as a testament to how following that message can impact our behavior and ultimately change our lives.

Jesus points out what a great responsibility it is to be salt and light to those around us. As we have seen, Jesus strongly rebukes hypocrites who claim to follow God and uphold his laws, but act completely contrary to his teachings. Jesus even said it would be better for someone to drown in the sea than for them to misrepresent the message of God (Luke 17:1). As ambassadors of God's kingdom, we are to let the light of the Spirit shine through us to represent the kingdom of God, its truth, and the impact it can have on the world.

What Impact Can We Make as Ambassadors of the Kingdom of God?

Jesus uses several parables to explain how we can impact the kingdom of God as we serve as its ambassadors during our life in this world. While there are times our message may be rejected, our efforts both big and small can have great impact on the world around us.

In the parable of the sower (Matthew 13:18–23; Mark 4:1–20; Luke 8:4–15), Jesus explains that the kingdom of God is like a farmer who plants his seeds. Some seeds may fall where they are quickly eaten by the birds. Some may fall on rocky ground where they sprout quickly, but cannot establish roots so wither and die. Some seeds fall amongst the thorn bushes, which choke out the young sprouts. Finally, some of the seeds will fall on good soil where they can grow and have the potential to produce a great harvest. Jesus explained that the message of the kingdom is like these seeds. Sometimes the message will produce great fruit, and other times it will not take root. Our job is simply to make sure the message is planted. The rest depends on the heart that receives it.

What Is Next for the Kingdom?

It is important to remember that today we experience the kingdom of God spiritually as we continue to physically live in a worldly kingdom. This spiritual kingdom will continue until Jesus comes back to earth to physically reclaim the kingdom of the world. In the meantime, those of us who live as spiritual citizens of the kingdom will have all the rights, privileges, and resources of the kingdom at our disposal.

In the Gospels of Matthew, Mark, and Luke, the authors record what Jesus says about the end of the worldly kingdom. Jesus emphasized that his purpose the first time he came to earth was to save people. The next time he comes to earth it will be to judge people (Matthew 24:3–51; Mark 13:3–37; Luke 21:7–38). The book of Revelation, the last book in the New Testament and written by the same author as the Gospel of John, explains the end of times when Jesus will return to earth to reclaim his creation.

While I am not going into much detail on this topic now, I would like to take a moment to share some of my thoughts on this subject. When Jesus comes to earth the second time it seems pretty clear that it will be to draw lines between those who have accepted his gift of salvation and those who have chosen to decline it. This message has always been a bit confusing to me. How can Jesus teach a message of love and acceptance and then turn around and judge people, essentially condemning them to hell? It all seems so counterintuitive and not very loving, Because this was such a source of confusion for me, I decided to unpack it a little further.

We have learned that God is the essence of perfect justice, but also of perfect love. How can these two characteristics be reconciled? If God requires punishment for sin, can that really be considered perfect love? As I thought about it more, a thought occurred to me. When Jesus came to earth and died on the cross, he provided us a way to satisfy God's justice, which was also an unbelievable act of love. The one requirement is that we have to accept that gift and follow him. If we choose not to accept that gift, the consequences of that are our own, not the act of an unloving God. Let me give you a scenario that might help explain it a little better.

Imagine that a father decided he was going to save enough money to pay off his children's student loans. He wanted his kids to be able to live free of that debt as they started families of their own. He saved for years and sacrificed many things in order to give his children this gift. He finally saved up enough money, called his children together, and presented each with enough money to pay off their debt. Two of his children immediately paid off their loans and very much enjoyed the comfort and freedom of living free and clear of that debt. The other two children decided they wanted to spend the money on other things. Their father was quite upset and considered forcefully imposing his will on them. But as much as he wanted his kids to be free of the debt, if he was truly giving them a gift, the decision had to be theirs. To force his will on them would only lead to resentment. The father decided that he loved them so much that he would let them ultimately decide what to do with the gift he offered them.

In a way, I think this scenario helps me answer my question. When Jesus comes to earth again, we could interpret his actions as judgment on those who chose not to follow him, or we could interpret his actions as respecting their decision not to follow him. It is a matter of perspective. It seems to me that God loves us so much that he will not force us to follow his will, but gives each and every one of us the right to hold our own destiny in our hands. That seems to me both perfect justice and perfect love.

Who Should We Pray To?

I would like to take just a moment to address another issue I have struggled with. We have seen in our studies that God encompasses three distinct individuals, God the Father, God the Son, and God the Holy Spirit. Together they are referred to as the Trinity. They are all coequal, fully divine, and eternal; and each plays an important and unique role. My question is this: Exactly who should we be working to establish a relationship with? To be honest, this is something I still find confusing and am still seeking to understand. It will definitely be a topic of study as I continue on in my journey. In the meantime, I think of it like this:

- God the Father is the father and creator of all that is. Jesus referred to him as, "Lord of heaven and earth" (Matthew 11:25). I find myself in awe of his power and glory every time I look at the stars, the oceans, the mountains, and the perfect beauty of nature. His brilliant creativity and abundant love are evident in all his creation, which includes you and me too!

- God the Son, Jesus, is described as the Son of God, and the Bible often refers to him as our brother. God the Father sent him to live on Earth to teach us how to live according to his will. Because Jesus lived on this earth, he can relate to our human emotions and the worldly challenges we face. Jesus willingly agreed to die a horrific death that he did not deserve to give us the opportunity to live forever in relationship with God. He reigns over God's kingdom and stands at the door, ready to welcome us.

- God the Holy Spirit provides us a connection to the kingdom and the Spirit's presence in us serves to indicate that we are no longer marked for death. We receive the Holy Spirit when we accept Jesus' sacrifice on our behalf and make a commitment to live according to the culture of God's kingdom. More about this shortly.

Conclusion

As I consider the message that Jesus delivered two thousand years ago it has become very clear to me that he came to reestablish God's kingdom government. He did not come to establish "religion." While many who promote and enforce the doctrines of religious beliefs may do so with good intent, it seems to me to be contrary to what Jesus himself intended. Jesus made it very clear that accepting his gift and living in God's kingdom is a choice. Once we make the choice to be citizens of his kingdom, we are to represent God's kingdom here on Earth. We have never been instructed to further define it or force it upon others. Our only job is to represent the culture of the kingdom and strive to live as witnesses to its truth.

PART V

APPLYING THE MESSAGE

PART V

APPLYING THE MESSAGE

Chapter 14

STAND

My journey thus far has been a series of questions. I began by exploring what evidence there is for the existence of God, then asking who is that God and what is his message to the world. I now find myself asking yet another question: What does God want from me?

To leave this an intellectual theory would make this journey a complete waste of time. Jesus told us we are to love God with our entire being which includes our mind, soul, and heart. I feel like I have done a fairly good job of intellectually proving God in my mind. The next step is to prove it to my heart. Honestly, I think this creates the biggest challenge for me. "Faith" has broken my heart before and left me feeling very lost. There is part of me that feels a little vulnerable as I take another leap into this faith thing. This time, however, I know it is different. This time I am not operating on blind faith or the forces of magnetic north. This time I have done my due diligence and have tried my best to find the truth. I guess you could say it is now time to field test it.

The first step of the field test is to find a way to apply the message of Jesus in my everyday life. Because I am easily distracted, I wanted to find an easy way to recall the instructions Jesus provided for successfully living in the kingdom. I also wanted to be reminded of what God promises as a result of implementing those instructions. Those promises provided me with a great deal of hope, but I also feel they can provide me some level of measurement to ensure that my results are in line with what God said to expect.

When I was back in law school and studying for the bar exam, I often used mnemonics to help me memorize important points. A mnemonic is a pattern of letters or words that help you remember something. I decided to give it a try to help me in this situation as well. I studied the lessons Jesus taught on living in the kingdom and came up with a list of daily considerations and actions and a list of expected results. I found two words that not only provided me those daily reminders but which have very special meaning and significance in my life. These two words are STAND and CLIMB.

The reason these words are special to me is that they immediately bring to mind thoughts of the mountains. The mountains will forever be my happy place and the place I feel most connected to God. The first thing you must do when you set out to hike or to summit a mountain is to take the effort to STAND. To STAND means you found the energy, courage, and determination to get up off your butt. The word STAND also means that you have taken a position or stance—that you have planted your feet firmly on the ground so that no one can easily push you off balance. The word STAND is my mnemonic representing what I want to do every day as a citizen of God's kingdom.

CLIMB is another important word in the mountains. Climbing is the process of moving toward the summit or your personal goal. In mountaineering, climbing takes a great deal of effort. The beauty about climbing in God's kingdom is that we only have to take the effort to STAND and he does all the climbing for us. Jesus said, "Come to me all who are weary and burdened and I will give you rest. . . . For my yoke is easy and my burden is light" (Matthew 11:28, 30). The word CLIMB is my mnemonic representing God's promises to those who choose to STAND as citizens in his kingdom. Let's spend this chapter looking at the first mnemonic: STAND.

S – Seek First the Kingdom of God

But seek first his kingdom and his righteousness,
and all these things will be given to you as well.
(Matthew 6:33)

As I have considered how to apply Jesus' instruction to seek first, I have found that there are three different stages of seeking God in life. The first is foundational seeking, the second kingdom seeking, and finally daily seeking. Let me explain.

Foundational seeking. Seeking foundation is taking the time to understand what you believe and why you believe it. It is essentially this journey we have trekked together.

Kingdom seeking. If the conclusion you have reached has brought you to the gates of the kingdom of God, the next step is to seek to enter. We don't have to come to those gates with a golden ticket, a perfect understanding, or a perfect faith. Jesus said to enter we must be born again through the process of repentance.

While that sounds a little mystical and frightening, it is not meant to be. We simply need to come to those gates with two things. The first is to come with our minds and hearts open to embracing Jesus and to accept the sacrifice of death that he paid on our behalf. Second, we need to come to the gates with a desire to change—to put the ways of the world behind us and focus on the ways of God's kingdom. If we stand at the gate with those two things, we will be warmly welcomed and God our Father will celebrate our return, just as the prodigal son was welcomed back to his father's house.

If you want to celebrate your entry into the kingdom as well, you might choose to be baptized. Typically, you would find a church community to help you with that process. If you do not belong to a church or want to find a new place to start, reach out to a friend who attends a church they respect and trust and see if it feels right to you. If nothing else, take some time to celebrate the choices you have made and just party with God, who is overjoyed that you have joined his kingdom.

Daily seeking: Once we are citizens of the kingdom, we will want to seek ways to prioritize the values of the kingdom while we continue to physically live in the kingdom of the world. This is not always an easy task. There are lots of shiny objects, relationships, and responsibilities in our daily lives that capture and even require our attention. We cannot ignore or neglect our relationships and responsibilities. I suspect that Jesus can very much relate to the conflict of trying to live in the world while being a citizen of God's kingdom. This is why he instructed us to seek the kingdom first. Jesus told us that if we approach all that we do seeking God first, the rest of life will fall into place. Now that doesn't mean that everything will always go exactly as planned or that we will not face challenges or even heartbreak. Because we live in an imperfect world, those things are always possible. What it does means is that if we intentionally and purposefully seek God first and to live according to the ways of his kingdom, he will help us manage everything else the world has to throw at us.

As we continue to explore how to STAND in the kingdom, we will discover more specific ways in which we can put God first.

T – Time

> Do not be anxious about anything, but in every situation, by
> prayer and petition, with thanksgiving, present your requests
> to God. (Philippians 4:6)

Time is one of the biggest parts of seeking God first every day. I have found that there are two different aspects of time that seem important: time to build relationship with God, and time to *allow* him the time to work in our lives.

Relationship time: Every day we must intentionally make time to establish a relationship with God. Like any other relationship in our life, it takes time to get to know each other and to trust each other. Those things can only happen on a very personal level over time. I used to automatically assume that time with God meant time praying. While that is not the only way to spend time with God, it is a great first step. Since we will be talking more about relationship with Jesus and the Holy Spirit shortly, I would like to focus here on ways in which we can specifically pray to God the Father.

When the disciples asked Jesus how to pray, he taught them the Lord's Prayer. While some repeat this as a rote prayer, I think it was more likely an example of a format we can use for prayer. Let's walk through the Lord's Prayer (Matthew 6:9–13) and see how we can use it for guidance during our time with God.

Our Father in heaven

Jesus is teaching us to have a personal conversation with God, in the same way you would a cherished father. In fact, the word Jesus uses in the original language is *abba*, which means "daddy." Jesus tells us to call out to God as a child would call out to her daddy who loves and protects her. Because Jesus refers to him as "our" Father, it is important to remember that we live in community with each other as brothers and sisters. We are all children of God.

Hallowed be your name

Jesus demonstrates that we should praise and thank God for what we have. Gratitude can be an extremely powerful human emotion. It often resets our mood, attitude, and outlook, and helps us ditch the bad mojo going on inside of us.

Your kingdom come, your will be done, on earth as it is in heaven.

Jesus reminds us of the spiritual kingdom of God that is available to us today and that there is an even greater kingdom to come. He explains that we should ask for help accomplishing

God's will in the earthly kingdom, just as it is in the heavenly kingdom.

Give us today our daily bread.

Jesus taught that if we seek God first every day, he will provide us with all we need. We do not have to be anxious or worry about having enough to eat, what to wear, or where to live. God will provide that for us. Jesus also taught that it is OK to ask God for help in accomplishing his will. He told us that if we ask, we will receive. It may not be done in our timing, but God will deliver it in his perfect timing in a much better way than we could have ever imagined.

And forgive us our debts, as we also have forgiven our debtors.

Jesus told us that we should strive to live according to the laws of the kingdom, but when we fail we should ask for God's forgiveness and his help to get back on track. As God forgives us, he also expects that we will forgive each other.

And lead us not into temptation, but deliver us from the evil one.

Jesus knows what it is like to live in a world full of temptations. He lived on Earth and was tempted by Satan himself. He knows we do not have enough strength on our own to deal with the temptations of the world, but promises that if we rely on God's strength we will always win.

Time in prayer is a wonderful way to connect with God and to learn more about who he is. Other ways we can do this is through Bible study, worship services, recited prayers, or just personal conversations with God. My personal goal is to learn more about something called "contemplative prayer." This practice emphasizes the benefits of rewiring your brain to live free of self-focused, worldly thinking and to focus on the pure joy of creation, being present in the "now" and living in relationship with God.[83] I am so excited to learn more!

Processing time. A second way that time is an important part of learning to STAND in the kingdom is by giving God time to work. In today's world we have become accustomed to instant gratification and solutions. That is not the way God works. Consider that God may need time to work through other people in order to help you accomplish your goals. He may also need you to see things from a different perspective or to make some necessary changes before he can fully answer your prayers. If we give up and abandon our hope before giving God time to work through the situation, we may never realize what blessings he had in store for us!

Ironically, the biggest challenge to finding time with God is not having enough time. Every day we have more than enough in terms of worldly commitments, responsibilities, and obligations to fill twenty-four hours. Trust me, as a single mom, maintaining a home, raising three girls, and working full time I get it! We all know that life is busy, time is short, and excuses are easy. You might try to get up a little earlier or cut back on some screen time, but sometimes all you have time to do is to make room for him to walk next to you during your busy day. It really boils down to an awareness of his presence every minute of the day.

A – Attitude of Altitude, Living Like Jesus

You call me "Teacher" and "Lord," and rightly so, for that is what I am. Now that I, your Lord and Teacher, have washed your feet, you also should wash one another's feet. I have set you an example that you should do as I have done for you. Very truly I tell you, no servant is greater than his master, nor is a messenger greater than the one who sent him. Now that you know these things, you will be blessed if you do them. (John 13:13–17)

One of the main messages Jesus taught during his ministry was how to live above the ways of the world. He taught us that living according to the values and culture of God's kingdom is very different than living according to the values and culture of the world. Jesus not only instructed us on how to live, but continuously demonstrated it in the way he lived his life. Every day we should strive to live like Jesus, above the hostility, hatred, materialistic, self-absorbed ways of the world. Here are some of the things we can do every day to live with an attitude of altitude like Jesus.

Surrender to God's will. Jesus knows the challenges we face as we continue to physically live in this world while trying to live spiritually in the kingdom of God. We can rely on him to help us surrender our will and to live rightly in the kingdom. He knows we do not have the power to do this in our own strength.

Love and serve each other. This all starts with being aware of opportunities. How many times have we seen others in need and not realized until later that we had the opportunity to help them? How many times have we just been too busy to find time for others, even those in our own family? We can love and serve others in small ways, such as simply taking the time to look a stranger in the eyes and to smile. We can love and serve others in big ways by assisting when people need help, or by just showing up during a time of need.

Be kind, gentle, and exercise self-control. It is easy to fall into worldly traps such as responding out of anger or frustration or just being rude because you are in a bad mood. Jesus taught us to act with kindness, no matter what our mood.

Promote equality and fight for justice. Everyone in the kingdom has equal value and is equally loved by God. This means that we are to have respect for everyone, regardless of whether they hold different religious and political views, whether they are poor or rich, popular or unpopular, have a different color skin or have different morals and values than we do. Jesus said we are to accept differences and never stand in judgment of each other. I have to admit that this one has caused me a great deal of confusion. I totally get the concept that we are all equal, but am confused as to how we are to reconcile our responsibility to fight for equality and justice—to stand up for what we believe in and to express concern for others—and at the same time avoid being judgmental, or what our society today would label as intolerant. Let me give you a couple quick scenarios to help illustrate my point:

- I am concerned that one of my friends has a drinking problem. I have observed on many occasions he drinks to the point of slurring his words and stumbling and have observed that his behavior has upset and often hurt others. I am also extremely concerned that at some point his excessive drinking will affect his health. Do I have a responsibility to talk to him about my concerns, or would expressing my opinion be judgmental?

- There is a discussion at work about religion. Someone expressed her opinion that all religions are equally correct and that no one religion should be considered "right." I explained that after many years of study, I have come to the personal conclusion that based on evidence and logic Jesus of Nazareth was the Son of God who came to Earth to offer us all forgiveness if we choose to accept it. I was told that I was being intolerant, which was unacceptable in the workplace.

Is there a distinction between judgment and intolerance on one hand and discernment concerning what is true or false, right or wrong, on the other? While I continue to struggle with this question, I believe the answer lies in how we approach and respond to *people*, versus how we approach and respond to *issues*. In terms of people, we are *never* to degrade, demean, or humiliate others regardless of what they believe or what they have done. Our job is never to judge people. We do, however, have the right—and sometimes even the responsibility—to discuss the issues. Of course, we need to discuss those issues in a spirit of respect. It seems to me that we as a society have a long way to go in terms of this type of discourse. I think we could all benefit from some tools or guidelines that could help us find ways to respectfully discuss the issues we face as a society without degrading each other.

Forgive others and be empathetic. Jesus told us we are to forgive others who hurt us and have empathy for those who are hurting. Empathy is the ability to identify and connect with someone who is hurting, to help when we can, and to let that person know he or she is not alone. While Jesus taught us to forgive and have empathy, it seems like another area where it is extremely important to have some boundaries. For example, is there a line between forgiveness and condoning abuse? Is there a line between being empathetic and being taken advantage of? Let's again look at a couple scenarios to help illustrate these points.

- My husband sometimes gets so mad that he says very hurtful things to me. He calls me names and on one occasion even physically hurt me. After he has time to calm down, I can tell he feels really bad and apologizes. Unfortunately, this behavior has become a pattern. Does forgiveness mean I am supposed to forget and "turn the other cheek," as Jesus said?

- My sister is having a really hard time dealing with depression. She cannot even seem to find the energy or desire to get out of bed some days. I told her that when she is having a really hard time, she should let me know and I would do my best to help her. For about a month now she has been asking me to do her chores and sometimes even her homework as she is feeling too depressed to do it. I feel really bad for her, but nothing seems to be getting any better and I am starting to feel used and resentful.

These scenarios illustrate some challenges when it comes to forgiveness and empathy. Jesus certainly never intended that we should forgive people to the point of accepting abuse. In fact, I don't think he ever suggested anything of the sort. Turning the other cheek does not literally mean that when someone hits us, we should let them hit us again.

It means that when someone offends us, we are not to take revenge or retribution, even if they offend us again. Forgiveness does not even necessarily mean that we have to make amends with the person who hurt us. People should rightly face the consequences of their behavior, which may result in the loss of relationship or even punishment if it rises to the level of a criminal offense. Forgiveness is much more about our attitude and letting go of hatred and resentment, as that tends to hurt us far more than it does the other person.

It is also very important that having empathy for someone does not turn into enabling him. We want to help and comfort people when they are hurting and do not have the ability or skills to help themselves. Most importantly we want to encourage them to find ways of coping, solutions, and tools to help themselves. If we end up continuously providing solutions for them, we prevent them from the opportunity to grow. Empathy should never involve doing for someone else what they should be doing for themselves.

Be sincere. When we serve and love others we must do it with sincerity. We cannot tell people that we care and then never show up or follow through. One of the things Jesus was adamant about is that we not be hypocritical, saying one thing and doing another. Insincerity and hypocrisy have the potential not only to hurt other people but to turn others away from the message of Jesus, particularly if you are hypocritical "Christian."

Plant seeds. As we strive to live like Jesus, we cannot expect to change anyone overnight, and we certainly cannot forcefully shove Jesus' message down anyone's throat. Jesus told us to plant the seeds of his word and the ways of the kingdom. He taught that even a tiny mustard seed has the potential to grow into a majestic tree. We are to be salt and light to the earth, demonstrating and shining light on what is right and good.

Living like Jesus is not easy. It is a process and something that we can only achieve over time and with practice. Jesus told us that he is always available to help us, and gives us the Holy Spirit to be present with us at all times.

N – Navigate with the Holy Spirit

But the Advocate, the Holy Spirit, whom the Father will send
in my name, will teach you all things and will remind you of
everything I have said to you. (John 14:26)

Another way in which we can STAND in the kingdom of God is to navigate our daily lives relying on the direction and guidance of the Holy Spirit. By the way, for some reason I always think of the Holy Spirit as a woman, likely because my mom has been such a source of guidance and love in my life. I imagine the Holy Spirit must be like a beautiful loving mother. Anyway, just my opinion, but one that I will employ in the following section.

I have been able to wrap my head around God as the Father and Jesus as the Son. I have context for their positions which make them relatable. I have a hard time, however, conceptualizing the role of the Holy Spirit in my life. It is something I will have to continue to study and seek to understand. An important point to note is that Jesus taught us that the Holy Spirit is a very big deal. He spoke of the strength, power, wisdom, and guidance the Spirit provided him during his ministry. If the Holy Spirit could provide those things to the Son of God, the lady must have it together! Jesus promised that same Spirit to his disciples and to you and me. I think it is worth the time to figure out how to harness that amazing power!

It seems to me that understanding the Holy Spirit is much more than learning or studying a biblical message. Understanding the Spirit seems to develop and grow through personal experience. Since I am still learning about the Spirit and how she works, I will share what I have discovered so far. This information is gathered from the authors of the New Testament, as well as, reports of other's personal experiences and just a few of my own.

What is the purpose of the Holy Spirit?

- The Bible tells us that the Holy Spirit dwells within us. I imagine her to be like our direct satellite connection to the kingdom. We are told in Paul's letter to the Romans that the Spirit will actually contact God for us when we don't know what to say or do (Romans 8:26).

- The presence of the Holy Spirit in us serves as a sign that we have been saved by the blood of Jesus. Perhaps she is the one who actually washes away that big giant X Satan used to mark us for death! When Jesus told us to let the light within us shine, he was likely referring to the light of the Holy Spirit. This light serves as a sign to others that we are a citizen of the kingdom.

- I think it is safe to say that the Holy Spirit is like our own personal GPS navigation system. She provides us direction when it comes to making important decisions, but more importantly provides us with insight into ways in which we can use the talents and gifts that God has given each one of us.

- Jesus describes the Holy Spirit as the "Spirit of truth," revealing to us truth, wisdom, and understanding. She serves as our helper, advocate, and teacher. The Holy Spirit provides us the strength, courage, and determination to live like Jesus since it is simply not possible under our own strength. By helping us live like Jesus she positions us to produce great "fruit" in the kingdom. More about this shortly.

- The Holy Spirit is our comforter when we are hurting, our counselor when we need advice, and our cheerleader when we need encouragement. Kind of like our own personal BFF!

Engaging the Holy Spirit. The Bible tells us to "walk with the Spirit" (Galatians 5:22). When I imagine walking with the Spirit, I literally picture her like my right-hand woman, there with me all the time. My experience has been that while she may be with us all the time, I do not always feel her presence. I am only able to feel her presence when I, for lack of a better analogy, plug in to her energy. Of course, that can happen during prayer, but I have come to realize that I can plug in at anytime and anywhere. I can plug in while I am hiking in the woods or driving in rush hour, when I am cleaning my house or in a business meeting. I can plug in in the midst of crisis or when I am celebrating success. She is there in all those moments. I just have to plug in! It is then I experience her guidance, wisdom, truth, insight, and power. I have definitely noticed that if I forget to plug in for a while or ignore her advice the connection gets a bit fuzzy. I have learned I really hate that feeling so try to be very conscious of her presence and my need to plug in at all times.

Hearing from the Spirit. So how do we know we are being guided or hearing from the Holy Spirit and not just acting on our own emotion or hearing from our conscience? Honestly, I don't know if there is a great answer to that; it is something I am still seeking to understand. For now, I have to rely on what others report as their experiences with the Holy Spirit and my own limited experience.

- The Holy Spirit will give us what are referred to as leadings or promptings. I believe I have just recently started to distinguish promptings of the Holy Spirit from my own thoughts. I can only describe it as something that gives me a great sense of clarity and conviction as opposed to a feeling of emotion. Here is a quick example: One morning I was really struggling to find information to help me better understand the Holy Spirit and how she works. I could not find answers to some of the questions I had. That very same morning I had gone into my closet to get something. For some reason I looked up at the top shelf and saw some books I had not paid attention to for a long time. One caught my eye. I crawled up to get it and opened it. I happened to open to a page where there was something circled. That page contained information that led me to an answer I had been searching for! I am totally not kidding. I carried that book around with me for the next several weeks, just because it felt comforting to have it near me.

- Other ways people report hearing from the Holy Spirit is by way of receiving what they call "inner" guidance or enlightenment.

Some say they have experienced visions, dreams, and other supernatural experiences. Since I have never experienced anything like this, I will leave it to you to explore reports of those experiences on your own if you are interested.

While I have known of the Holy Spirit all my life, having her as part of my life is still very new to me. I know that she is a very important element to being able to STAND in the kingdom. I will continue to study and learn ways in which I can use her guidance and power to help me navigate through life. I must say, it is completely amazing to me that the Holy Spirit who knows the thoughts and heart of God is available to personally help me navigate life!

D – Do It!

What good is it, my brothers and sisters, if someone claims
to have faith but has no deeds? Can such faith save them?
Suppose a brother or a sister is without clothes and daily
food. If one of you says to them, "Go in peace; keep warm
and well fed," but does nothing about their physical needs,
what good is it? In the same way, faith by itself, if it is not
accompanied by action, is dead. (James 2:14–17)

The last thing we must do each day to STAND in the kingdom is to actually do what God has asked us to do as citizens of his kingdom. While we do not have to earn citizenship, we are expected to participate as citizens of God's kingdom community. Remember earlier that we talked about our role as being like that of an ambassador. We are citizens of the kingdom of God, but representing his government while living in the kingdom of the world.

Most of what we can accomplish as ambassadors for the kingdom does not require a ton of preparation or planning. We are primarily called to love God with our whole being and to serve and love others in the way Jesus taught us. Much of that can be accomplished by simply being aware of opportunities to serve others. When you begin to look for them you will find them!

- The person in line ahead of you at the grocery store is short $10.
- A young gal is sitting in her stalled car in the middle of a four-way stop intersection.
- A blind man at the airport struggles to find a place to sit while waiting at the gate.
- You find a wallet someone dropped.
- Your niece is struggling at school.
- A homeless person approaches you while you are having lunch in the park.
- Your dad needs help figuring out the internet.
- The neighbor that has been rude to you in the past waves hi.
- A friend hurts you.
- A tornado demolishes a small town near you.

While I could go on, I am guessing you get the picture. There are opportunities all around us, but we have to be watching for them and be ready to *do*! The challenging part of serving and loving is not that there are not enough opportunities; the problem is that we can always find an excuse not to help. Sometimes those excuses are legitimate. Time, resources, and ability always have to be considerations. There have also been times I have hesitated to help someone, fearing I will offend them. I have also been reluctant to help when I feel there is a possibility of making myself vulnerable and falling prey to someone who has bad intentions. These are all valid concerns, at which point we plug in to the Holy Spirit and ask for her help. It is amazing what she can do to help you find solutions!

Chapter 15

CLIMB

Now that we have covered what it takes to STAND each day in the kingdom of God, let's talk about the expected results. We cannot think of these things in terms of reimbursement for our efforts or what you "deserve" in return. We should think about them in terms of what we can expect when our efforts to STAND are hitting the mark. If we are not experiencing these things, we might want to reevaluate and reassess our efforts. Here is my understanding of what it means to CLIMB in the kingdom.

C – Continued Challenge

Therefore, since we have been justified through faith, we have peace with God through our Lord Jesus Christ, through whom we have gained access by faith into this grace in which we now stand. And we boast in the hope of the glory of God. Not only so, but we also glory in our sufferings, because we know that suffering produces perseverance; perseverance, character; and character, hope. (Romans 5:1–4)

I am guessing that challenge is not the first thing you expected to find as you take a STAND in the kingdom of God. The reason it is important to expect it is because it will continue to occur. We cannot interpret continued challenge as a rejection of God's love and abandon the fight. Jesus told us there would be challenges. Being an ambassador and citizen of the kingdom does not mean we are immune from the challenges of this world. What God promised is that he will use all of the challenges we face and turn them into good. "And we know that in all things God works for the good of those who love them, who have been called according to his purpose" (Romans 8:28).

Some of the most common reasons people give for turning away from God are things like disappointment, difficulties, unrealistic expectations, discouragement, and doubt. They ask, "How could a good God allow such terrible things to happen to good people?" It only takes a few words to stir up emotion on this subject: cancer, war, rape, child abuse, terrorism, murder, hunger, discrimination, depression, poverty, addiction, hatred, suicide, natural disasters, COVID-19. Are you feeling the emotion? Why does it happen? I am not going to pretend to know the answer, because I don't. I can, however, tell you what the Bible says.

While we are spiritual citizens of the kingdom of God, we live in a world that is being governed by an evil and corrupt governor. He leads a government system with its main goal to promote rebellious opposition to God. While Satan does not now nor will he ever own the earthly kingdom or have ultimate authority over it, he does have a certain degree of power as its current governor. Satan is currently and will continue to deceive and lie to people, keeping them hostage to sin and death and preventing them from gaining citizenship to the kingdom. As people, who possess free will, continue to choose his way over God's way, there will continue to be evil in this world.

The great news is that there is a difference between power and authority. Satan may have temporary power in this world, but he does not have final authority. Jesus has already taken the first step to defeat him. His death on the cross created the opportunity for us to live today in the kingdom of God. In my opinion, it is unfair and inaccurate to criticize God for not doing anything about the evil in this world. He has! He sent his Son into this world to show us the right way. It is our job to follow him and ask him to help us change the world. As I sit here in the midst of a worldwide COVID-19 pandemic, it is amazing to see what people can do when they choose to help others in need. The COVID crisis has been a clear example of what people, in the midst of fear and tragedy, can do to help and support each other and change the world. I imagine that makes God smile.

There is another reason why we will continue to experience challenges, even after we become citizens of the kingdom. There may be times that God needs to strengthen us. Just like hitting the gym, we have to work and tear our muscles to experience growth and strength. God may also be telling us he needs us to trust him more, to lean on his strength and not our own. He may want to prove to us that we can step into the fire but not be burned. Sometimes God sends us a good old-fashioned challenge because it is the only way he can get us to slow down to hear his voice.

Remember I told you that I found a book on the shelf in my closet? After struggling for a long time to understand how God could allow us to struggle and face such extreme challenges, this is the message I found circled in that book: "Life is an interpretive experience. What happens is less important than how we respond to our circumstances."[84] This sentence put the idea of challenge into a whole new perspective for me. It reminded me that this life and the world we currently live in is imperfect. There will always be "circumstances" to deal with; however, circumstances are not what we are to focus on or be concerned about. What we are to focus on is our reactions to those circumstances. The world will hand us some bad situations, but as ambassadors representing the kingdom of God, we have the potential to turn the worst evil into the most amazing good.

L – Life Abundantly and Eternally

And God is able to bless you abundantly, so that in all things
at all times, having all that you need, you will abound in every
good work. (2 Corinthians 9:8)

The word "abundant" in Greek is *perisson*; it means "beyond measure"
or "exceedingly." Jesus promises that as citizens of the kingdom we will
have a life far beyond what we could ever imagine. This does not mean
that we are necessarily going to be exceedingly wealthy, live in a mansion,
or drive a Ferrari. Remember that these things are not important in the
kingdom of God. God promises we will experience life abundantly, not
to have abundance. Let's look at what that means.

- First and foremost, we know that as citizens of the kingdom we
  are guaranteed the gift of eternal life. The death of Jesus has provided a way to wash away the mark of death.

- God promised that if we seek first the kingdom of God each day,
  he will always provide us what we need in terms of food and water
  and a place to live. We can take that off the list of worries.

- We are promised the peace and power of the spiritual kingdom
  of God as we live out our life on earth. That kingdom is available
  to us the minute we accept the sacrifice of Jesus and commit to
  change. With citizenship in the kingdom comes the gift of the
  Holy Spirit. Through the Spirit we have the power and resources
  of the kingdom at our disposal every minute of every day. More
  on what the Holy Spirit offers us in just a minute.

- The Beatitudes also tell us that we will receive the abundant blessings of comfort, satisfaction, and mercy as we live in the kingdom.
  That covers a lot of bases if you think about it.

  - Comfort means feeling happy and safe. It means living free
    from anxiety and the suffocating pressures of the world

around us. Comfort also means feeling loved by God and by others.

> Satisfaction is the emotion we feel when we have successfully used our talents to accomplish something good. It is what we feel when we have good, strong, healthy relationships. It is also something we feel when we are content. So often contentment is consumed by the desire to acquire more and more stuff. Contentment is focused on what is inside of us, not by what we possess.

> Mercy is feeling value and self-worth even if we don't feel we deserve it. It is living free of the chains of guilt that can weigh us down and keep us from moving on to the person we are meant to be. Mercy is living as a transformed person in an imperfect world.

I – Insight and Fruits of the Spirt

I am the vine; you are the branches. If you remain in me and
I in you, you will bear much fruit; apart from me you can
do nothing. (John 15:5)

The insight and fruits of the Spirit are the blessings that the Holy Spirit brings to our life. Insight is what we gain through the guidance and wisdom of the Spirit. It is also our ability to recognize those little nudges and to act as representatives of God in the kingdom of the world.

The fruit of the Spirit (Galatians 5:22–23) are essentially what we will project to others as we let the Holy Spirit shine through us. From this fruit we will plant seeds in others that God will nurture and grow. This fruit includes:

- love
- joy

- peace
- patience
- kindness
- goodness
- faithfulness
- gentleness
- self-control

What a blessing we can be to other people if we can share these things with them.

M – My Significance and Purpose

And we know that in all things God works for the good of those who love him, who have been called according to his purpose. (Romans 8:28)

This one touches my heart in a very special place. At the very beginning of our journey together I shared that all my life I have had an overwhelming need to find purpose, meaning, and significance. No matter how hard I tried I could not find it and as a result found myself feeling very lost. Unfortunately, it seems that many people in our society today are finding themselves in the same situation. The confusion and uncertainty of what people describe as "feeling lost in life" manifests itself in crippling ways. Despite living in one of the most privileged and technologically advanced societies in the world, each year nearly 40 million Americans (18% of the population) suffer from anxiety-related disorders and depression affects another 17.3 million (7% of the population).[85] Sadly, many of those people become part of other statistics like the 19.7 million Americans who struggle with substance abuse,[86] the 1.4 million people who attempt to commit suicide each year, and the nearly 48,000 who succeed.[87]

It appears that all of us, regardless of our age, gender, race, socio-economic class, or any other life status, are equally at risk for getting lost. Teenagers find themselves lost as they struggle to fit in with their peers. Young adults find themselves lost as they try to determine what to do with their lives. People reaching middle age find themselves lost as they attempt to find meaning in life before it is too late. And golden-agers find themselves lost as they increasingly find themselves unappreciated and irrelevant to the world around them. No one is immune.

God has established a very clear plan and purpose for his human creation. We were made in the image of God to represent him as ambassadors of the kingdom of God on this amazing planet we call Earth. We are each valued and loved by the creator of this universe as his children and he desires to live in relationship with us for eternity. I cannot think of a greater or more important purpose.

B – Boldness and Strength

After they prayed, the place where they were meeting was
shaken. And they were all filled with the Holy Spirit and
spoke the word of God boldly. (Acts 4:31)

Finally, as we STAND in the kingdom of God we can expect to live with boldness and strength. We don't have to be afraid that we are not strong enough, smart enough, or good enough. We have the power of the Holy Spirit and the resources of the kingdom of God available to us every minute of every day. We can feel confident and bold about what we believe because we have taken the time to prove to ourselves the truth which we can support with evidence. There is nothing that should stop us from sharing what we know to be true.

Chapter 16

TRUE NORTH

Seven years ago, I started this journey at the very lowest point of my life, in a place I not so affectionately refer to as the pit. I can honestly say it is the scariest place I have ever been, and a place to which I will never return. Certainly, my own choices and many WTF moments contributed to launching me into that pit. (Please do me a favor: watch out for those WTF moments, avoid them where you can, but forgive yourself when they happen. We all have them!) But what ultimately left me lying at the bottom of that pit and completely without hope was the fact that faith and God appeared to have failed me. I know now that I had been misguided by blind faith and pointed in the wrong direction. My compass had been navigating me toward magnetic north and the forces of worldly elements which had caused fear, misunderstanding, uneducated allegiance, deception, and ignorance to creep into my life and my soul.

That rusty old blind-faith compass almost caused me to give up on God and faith altogether, but God had a different plan for me. It was not a plan I would have chosen. This was a long and challenging journey and by far the most difficult thing I have ever done in my life. I used to think climbing mountains was hard, but the challenges of climbing mountains are nothing compared to the falls I have taken, the roadblocks I have hit, the doubt I faced, and the exhaustion I have had to overcome as I struggled to complete this journey.

It turns out there was a brilliant silver lining to that pit I started out in. The pain of that pit caused me to ask some tough questions. Answering those questions pointed me in a new direction. I thought studying science would kill me, but ultimately it helped me find evidence to logically support the conclusion that there is an intelligent designer at work in our universe. It may not technically be considered a "scientific" conclusion, but I believe it is a logical conclusion.

The answer to that question caused me to ask another question: Who is God? The world's religions provide a lot of different answers to that question, but historical evidence supports only one answer. Jesus of Nazareth lived on this earth, died on a cross, and was resurrected to life again. Those historically reliable facts lead me to the logical conclusion that Jesus was God.

We then studied the message that God sent to the world which is presented in the Old and New Testaments. While the Bible may not be an academically satisfactory treatise with proper footnote references and editorial enhancements, it does provide us with a clear message. Its message of the kingdom provides us direction on how we can access the kingdom of God and find abundant life as we live out our life on earth and the opportunity to live in personal relationship with God for eternity. It has been a long journey, but a very rewarding finish.

I want to thank the abundance of loving, caring, and supportive family and friends in my life who believed in me even when I did not believe in myself. They have been and continue to be the best part of my life. I also want to thank you for taking the time to walk through this journey with me. I want you to know that I will pray for you regardless of your own personal conclusion. You may have found that after considering the facts and weighing the evidence you have reached different conclusions than I have. Please know, I completely respect that! The time you took to open your mind to ideas, to consider and analyze the evidence, and to reach conclusions for yourself is to be celebrated no matter what your ultimate conclusion.

I do ask one favor, though. I would ask that if you find there are questions I failed to consider or feel that my facts or logic are incorrect, that you continue to find answers for yourself. Don't give up until you understand what you believe and why you believe it. I would also truly love to learn more about what you find and the opportunity to dialogue on the issues (of course, while maintaining love and respect for each other as people!). This is certainly not the end of the journey for me. I plan to continue to learn and to explore the kingdom of God with the goal of finding truth and understanding for as long as I live on this earth.

Before I go, I would like to tell you a little bit about my life since I crawled out of that pit. Since that time, my baby girls have become young ladies. They have all finished college; two have opened their own businesses and one is in graduate school. Every day I thank God for the wonderful women they have become despite the crap I put them through.

As you know, my personal relationships in the past had been a four-teen-carat mess. I had pretty much given up on love and was content to live my life solo—until I met the most amazing and wonderful man I have ever known. He is kind, generous, patient, and amazingly talented. We are now married, and as a bonus I am blessed to add his beautiful family to my own. I thank God for that man every day.

Recently I left my twenty-four-year career as an attorney to start a new career. I am now a licensed contractor. My special guy and I have started our own contracting business and want to focus on helping those with disabilities make modifications to their homes to accommodate their unique special needs. I never imagined this is what I would do when I finally grew up, but I absolutely love it.

Perhaps the most important thing I discovered along this journey is the sense of purpose, meaning, and significance I have been searching for all my life. Believe it or not, I now see that the purpose of my life is to wander. I plan to live my life as a wandering ambassador of God's kingdom. I plan to *seek* first and prioritize the culture of God's kingdom, to spend *time* every day in relationship with the King, to live with an *attitude* of altitude like Jesus, to plug in to the Holy Spirit and *navigate* life under her guidance, and to *do* it all boldly planting the seeds of God's message while serving and loving others.

The most ironic thing about my journey is that I now find myself appreciating that old rusty compass, as in the end it helped me find the courage to begin this journey, the answers I needed to STAND, the grace to CLIMB, and ultimately set me in the direction of true north. I pray the same for you, my friend!

ENDNOTES

[1] GIS Geography, "Magnetic North vs Geographic (True) North Pole," GIS-Geography.com, https://gisgeography.com/magnetic-north-vs-geographic-true-pole (accessed March 29, 2020).

[2] Trevor Nace, "Earth's Magnetic North Pole Has Officially Moved (toward Russia)," *Forbes*, December 17, 2019, https://www.forbes.com/sites/trevor-nace/2019/12/17/earths-magnetic-north-pole-has-officially-moved-toward-russia/#323af13201fe (accessed March 29, 2020).

[3] Bryan Nelson, "Magnetic North Shifting by 30 Miles a Year, Might Signal Pole Reversal," Mother Nature Network, https://www.mnn.com/earth-matters/climate-weather/stories/magnetic-north-shifting-by-40-miles-a-year-might-signal-pole-r (accessed March 28, 2020).

[4] s.v. "faith," Merriam-Webster.com, https://www.merriam-webster.com/dictionary/faith (accessed March 30, 2020).

[5] Good resources on the Big Bang Theory:

- Jonathan Strickland, "How the Big Bang Theory Works," HowStuffWorks, https://science.howstuffworks.com/dictionary/astronomy-terms/big-bang-theory.htm (accessed March 30, 2020).

- All About Science. "Big Bang Theory," https://www.big-bang-theory.com (accessed March 30, 2020).

[6] "Thermodynamics," Physics for Idiots, http://physicsforidiots.com/physics/thermodynamics/ (accessed March 30, 2020).

[7] Good resources on quantum physics:

- Robert Adler, "Why Is There Something Rather Than Nothing?" BBC, http://www.bbc.com/earth/story/20141106-why-does-anything-exist-at-all (accessed March 31, 2020).

- Paul Anlee, "Could a 'Virtual Particle Chaos' Explain the Origins of the Universe?," https://www.paulanlee.com/2016/08/01/could-a-virtual-particle-chaos-explain-the-origin-of-the-universe (accessed March 31, 2020).

- Gordon Kane, "Are Virtual Particles Really Constantly Popping in and out of Existence? Or Are They Merely a Mathematical Bookkeeping Device for Quantum Mechanics?" *Scientific American*, https://www.scientificamerican.com/article/are-virtual-particles-rea (accessed March 31, 2020).

[8] Robert Nadis, "What Came before the Big Bang," *Discover Magazine*, https://www.discovermagazine.com/the-sciences/what-came-before-the-big-bang (accessed March 31, 2020).

[9] Terry Mortenson, "Young-Earth Creationist View Summarized and Defended," 1:1 Answers in Genesis, https://answersingenesis.org/creationism/young-earth/young-earth-creationist-view-summarized-and-defended/ (accessed March 31, 2020).

[10] Good resources on physical constants within the universe:

- Ethan Siegel, "It Takes 26 Fundamental Constants to Give Us Our Universe, but They Still Don't Give Everything," *Forbes*, August 22, 2015, https://www.forbes.com/sites/ethansiegel/2015/08/22/it-takes-26-fundamental-constants-to-give-us-our-universe-but-they-still-dont-give-everything/#5ea7543c4b86 (accessed September 27, 2020).

- David Bailey, "Is the Universe Fine-Tuned for Intelligent Life?" *Math Scholar*, https://mathscholar.org/2017/04/is-the-universe-fine-tuned-for-intelligent-life (accessed March 31, 2020).

[11] Good resources about planet Earth:

- Michael Greshko, "Planet Earth Explained," *National Geographic*, https://www.nationalgeographic.com/science/space/solar-system/earth (accessed March 31, 2020).

- Stephanie Pappas and Robert Roy Britt, "50 Interesting Facts about Earth," *Live Science*, https://www.livescience.com/19102-amazing-facts-earth.html (accessed March 31, 2020).

[12] Good resources on DNA:

- NA Diagnostics Center, "Understanding DNA in 10 Minutes," https://dnacenter.com/blog/understanding-dna-in-10-minutes/m   (accessed March 31, 2020).
- Helen Santoro, "Understanding DNA: The Layman's Guide," *Genetics Digest*, https://www.geneticsdigest.com/understanding-dna-the-laymans-guide (accessed March 31, 2020).
- Hannah Ashworth, "How Long Is Your DNA?" *Science Focus*, https://www.sciencefocus.com/the-human-body/how-long-is-your-dna (accessed April 1, 2020).

[13] Good resources for information on the brain:

- Liqun Luo. "Why Is the Human Brain So Efficient?" *Nautilus*, http://nautil.us/issue/59/connections/why-is-the-human-brain-so-efficient (accessed March 31, 2020).
- Tanya Lewis, "Human Brain: Facts, Functions & Anatomy," *Live Science*, https://www.livescience.com/29365-human-brain.html (accessed March 31, 2020).

[14] Good resources concerning detection of intelligence and information:

- Stephen Meyer, "Yes, Intelligent Design Is Detectable by Science," *Evolution News & Science Today*, https://evolutionnews.org/2018/04/yes-intelligent-design-is-detectable-by-science (accessed April 1, 2020).
- Stephen Meyer and Douglas Axe, "The Information Enigma—Where Does Information Come From?" Discovery Institute, https://www.discovery.org/v/the-information-enigma (accessed April 1, 2020).

[15] Good resources on probability of fine-tuning in the universe:

- Casey Luskin, "Roger Penrose on Cosmic Fine-Tuning: 'Incredible Precision in the Organization of the Initial Universe,'" *Evolution News & Science Today*, https://evolutionnews.org/2010/04/roger_penrose_on_cosmic_finetu (accessed March 31, 2020).

- "Teleological Argument and Entropy," All About Philosophy, https://www.allaboutphilosophy.org/teleological-argument-and-entropy-faq.htm (accessed April 1, 2020).

- Ralph Epperson, "How Did the Universe Begin?" Does God Exist, https://www.doesgodexist.org/JanFeb05/HowDidTheUniverseBegin.html (accessed March 31, 2020).

[16] Good resources of information on specified complexity:

- Peter Williams, "The Design Inference from Specified Complexity Defended by Scholars Outside the Intelligent Design Movement," Evangelical Philosophical Society, https://epsociety.org/library/articles.asp?pid=54&ap=1 (accessed April 1, 2020).

- Casey Luskin, "Intelligent Design (ID) Has Scientific Merit Because it Uses the Scientific Method to Make its Claims and Infers Design by Testing it Positive Predictions," Discovery Institute, https://www.discovery.org/a/7051 (accessed April 1, 2020).

[17] Good resources of information on the Cambrian explosion:

- Stephen Meyer and Douglas Axe, "The Information Enigma."

- *Evolution News & Science Today*, "In Cambrian Explosion Debate, ID Wins by Default." https://evolutionnews.org/2018/12/in-cambrian-explosion-debate-id-wins-by-default (accessed April 2, 2020).

[18] Good resources of information about micro vs. macro evolution:

- Understanding Evolution—Berkeley, "Evolution at Different Scales: Micro to Macro," https://evolution.berkeley.edu/evolibrary/article/0_0_0/evoscales_01 (accessed April 2, 2020).

- Henry Morris, "The Scientific Case against Evolution," Institute for Creation Research, https://www.icr.org/home/resources/resources_tracts_scientificcaseagainstevolution (accessed April 2, 2020).

[19] Good resources for an overview of the intelligent design theory:

- Stephen Meyer, "A Scientific History—and Philosophical Defense—of the Theory of Intelligent Design," Intelligentdesign.org, https://intelligentdesign.org/id/introductory/a-scientific-history-and-philosophical-defense-of-the-theory-of-intelligent-design (accessed April 2, 2020).

- *Evolution News & Science Today*, "Intelligent Design and Methodological Naturalism—No Necessary Contradiction," https://evolutionnews.org/2017/09/intelligent-design-and-methodological-naturalism-no-necessary-contradiction (accessed April 2, 2020).
- Stephen Meyer, "Philosopher of Science Stephen C. Meyer Explores the Exciting Theory of Intelligent Design," YouTube video, 1:00:45, February 27, 2019, https://www.youtube.com/watch?v=tu93Mw4mtec.

[20] Good resources for an overview of chemical evolution:

- Heather Scoville, "Understanding Chemical Evolution," ThoughtCo., https://www.thoughtco.com/understanding-chemical-evolution-1224538 (accessed April 2, 2020).
- Kahn Academy, "Hypotheses about the Origins of Life," https://www.khanacademy.org/science/biology/history-of-life-on-earth/history-life-on-earth/a/hypotheses-about-the-origins-of-life (accessed April 2, 2020).

[21] Good resources on the theory of evolution and natural selection:

- Ker Than, "What Is Darwin's Theory of Evolution?" LiveScience, https://www.livescience.com/474-controversy-evolution-works.html (accessed April 2, 2020).
- "Theory of Evolution," *National Geographic*, https://www.nationalgeographic.org/encyclopedia/theory-evolution (accessed April 2, 2020).
- Kahn Academy, "Darwin, Evolution & Natural Selection," https://www.khanacademy.org/science/biology/her/evolution-and-natural-selection/a/darwin-evolution-natural-selection (accessed April 2, 2020).

[22] Good resources on transitional fossils:

- Understanding Evolution, "Lines of Evidence: The Science of Evolution." https://evolution.berkeley.edu/evolibrary/article/_0_0/lines_01 (accessed April 2, 2020).
- Robin Lloyd, "Fossils Reveal Truth about Darwin's Theory," Live Science, https://www.livescience.com/3306-fossils-reveal-truth-darwin-theory.html (accessed April 2, 2020).

[23] Good resources on DNA as evidence for evolution:

- National Academy of Sciences, "Science and Creationism: A View from the National Academy of Sciences: Second Edition," https://www.ncbi.nlm.nih.gov/books/NBK230201/ (accessed April 2, 2020).

- Joe Hanson, "Proof of Evolution is in Your DNA," Science Connected Magazine, https://magazine.scienceconnected.org/2019/10/proof-of-evolution-is-in-your-dna (accessed April 2, 2020).

[24] Good resources on multiverse and fine-tuning.

- Craig Rusbult, "The Anthropic Principal: Is Fine Tuning of Nature Due to Multiverse and/or Intelligent Design?" The American Scientific Affiliation, https://www.asa3.org/ASA/education/origins/anthropic-cr.htm (accessed April 2, 2020).

- Victor Stenger, "Fine-Tuning and the Multiverse," *Skeptic*, https://www.skeptic.com/reading_room/fine-tuning-and-the-multiverse (accessed April 2, 2020),

[25] Good resources on naturalism and evolution:

- Richard Carrier, "My Journey into Naturalism." Cosmos Minutes, YouTube video, 19:15, February 16, 2018, https://www.youtube.com/watch?v=d3so02NW6_Q.

- John Rennie, "15 Answers to Creationists Nonsense," *Scientific American*, https://www.scientificamerican.com/article/15-answers-to-creationist/ (accessed April 2, 2020).

[26] Good resources on "God of the gaps" arguments:

- James Rochford, "Design and God of the Gaps." Evidence Unseen, http://www.evidenceunseen.com/articles/science-and-scripture/what-about-the-god-of-the-gaps/ (accessed April 2, 2020).

- Luke Muehlhauser, "Naturalism of the Gaps," Common Sense Atheism, http://commonsenseatheism.com/?p=9321 (accessed April 2, 2020).

[27] Great debates and discussions on topics of the existence of God, the universe, and life.

- "Unbelievable," "Lennox vs. Atkins—Can science explain everything?" YouTube video, 1:38:58. February 17, 2019, https://www.youtube.com/watch?v=fSYwCaFkYno.

- Capturing Christianity, "Did the Universe Begin to Exist? William Lane Craig vs. Alex Malpass," YouTube video, 2:05:08, March 24, 2020, https://www.youtube.com/watch?v=uWo9qU2dhpQ.

- Wycliffe College at the University of Toronto, "Krauss, Meyer, Lamoureux: What's Behind it all? God, Science and the Universe," YouTube video, 2:26:46. March 19, 2016. https://www.youtube.com/watch?v=mMuy58DaqOk.

- Larry King CNN, "Stephen Hawking, Leonard Mlodinow, Deepak Chopra and Father Robert Spitzer," YouTube video, 39:57, August 1, 2016, https://www.youtube.com/watch?v=_24sWyHvyxM.

[28] s.v. "scientific method," Merriam-Webster.com, https://www.merriam-webster.com/dictionary/scientific%20method (accessed April 3, 2020).

[29] Maggie Koerth, "How Do We Know When a Hunk of Rock Is Actually a Stone Tool?" FiveThirtyEight, https://fivethirtyeight.com/features/how-do-we-know-when-a-hunk-of-rock-is-actually-a-stone-tool (accessed April 2, 2020).

[30] Good resources on material naturalism:

- "Material Naturalism," Window View—Science, https://www.windowview.org/sci/pgs/38mat.naturl.a.html (accessed April 3, 2020).

- "Worldview Naturalism," Naturalism.org, https://www.naturalism.org/worldview-naturalism (accessed April 3, 2020).

[31] Good resources on critical thinking skills.

- S. M. Rayhanul, "What Are the Importance and Benefits of 'Critical Thinking Skills?'" LinkedIn, https://www.linkedin.com/pulse/what-importance-benefits-critical-thinking-skills-islam (accessed April 4, 2020).

- Lumen, "Chapter 7: Critical Thinking and Evaluating Information," https://courses.lumenlearning.com/austincc-learningframeworks/chapter/chapter-7-critical-thinking-and-evaluating-information/ (accessed April 4, 2020).

[32] s.v. "religion," Merriam-Webster.com, https://www.merriam-webster.com/dictionary/religion (accessed April 4, 2020).

[33] Good resources on world religions:

- World Economic Forum, "These Are All the World's Major Religions in One Map," https://www.weforum.org/agenda/2019/03/this-is-the-best-and-simplest-world-map-of-religions/ (accessed April 4, 2020).

- Pew Research Center, "The Global Religious Landscape," https://assets.pewresearch.org/wp-content/uploads/sites/11/2014/01/global-religion-full.pdf (accessed April 4, 2020).

[34] Good resources on Hinduism:

- "Hinduism," History.com, https://www.history.com/topics/religion/hinduism (accessed April 4, 2020).

- "Hinduism," Ancient History Encyclopedia, https://www.ancient.eu/hinduism (accessed April 4, 2020).

[35] Good resources on Buddhism:

- James Rochford, "Buddhism," Evidence Unseen, http://www.evidenceunseen.com/world-religions/buddhism (accessed April 4, 2020).

- PBS, "Basics of Buddhism," https://www.pbs.org/edens/thailand/buddhism.htm (accessed April 4, 2020).

[36] Good resources on Judaism:

- Menachem Posner, "Who Was Abraham? First Patriarch in the Bible," Chabad.org, https://www.chabad.org/library/article_cdo/aid/112356/jewish/Who-Was-Abraham-The-First-Patriarch-in-the-Bible.htm (accessed April 4, 2020).

- "About the Jewish Religion," Israel.org, http://www.israel.org/MFA/AboutIsrael/Spotlight/Pages/About%20the%20Jewish%20Religion.aspx (accessed April 4, 2020).

[37] Good resources on Christianity:

- "Christianity," History.com, https://www.history.com/topics/religion/history-of-christianity (accessed April 4, 2020).

- "Christianity," Religion Facts, http://www.religionfacts.com/christianity (accessed April 4, 2020).

[38] Good resources on Islam:

- Islam-Guide.com, "A Brief Illustrated Guide to Understanding Islam," https://www.islam-guide.com (accessed April 4, 2020).

- Daniel Peterson, "Understanding Islam," BYU Religious Studies Center, https://rsc.byu.edu/mormons-muslims/understanding-islam (accessed April 4, 2020).

[39] J. P. Moreland, "The Historicity of the New Testament," Bethinking, https://www.bethinking.org/is-the-bible-reliable/the-historicity-of-the-new-testament (accessed April 6, 2020).

[40] Zondervan Academic Blog, "Who Wrote the Gospels and How Do We Know for Sure?" https://zondervanacademic.com/blog/who-wrote-gospels (accessed April 6, 2020).

[41] Christian Think Tank, "Contradictions in the Infancy Stories," http://christianthinktank.com/infancyoff.html (accessed April 6, 2020).

[42] Michael Patton, "Eight Reasons Why the Gospels Are Embarrassing," Credohouse.org, https://credohouse.org/blog/why-the-gospels-are-embarrassing (accessed April 6, 2020).

[43] Bob Seidensticker, "25,000 New Testament Manuscripts? Big Deal," *Patheos*, https://www.patheos.com/blogs/crossexamined/2013/11/25000-new-testament-manuscripts-big-deal/ (accessed April 6, 2020).

[44] Josh McDowell and Clay Jones, "The Bibliographical Test," Equip.org, https://www.josh.org/wp-content/uploads/Bibliographical-Test-Update-08.13.14.pdf (accessed April 6, 2020).

[45] Bible Odyssey, "A History of the Text of the New Testament," https://www.bibleodyssey.org/en/tools/timeline-gallery/h/history-of-the-text-of-the-new-testament (accessed April 6, 2020).

[46] McDowell and Jones, "The Bibliographical Test."

[47] Evidence Unseen, "Bibliographical Test," http://www.evidenceunseen.com/theology/scripture/historicity-of-the-nt/1-bibliographical-test/ (accessed April 7, 2020).

[48] Alisa Childers, "3 Textual Variants Every Christian Should Know About," https://www.alisachilders.com/blog/3-textual-variants-every-christian-should-know-about (accessed April 7, 2020).

[49] Christopher Price, "Did Josephus Refer to Jesus? A Thorough Review of the Testimonium Flavianum," http://www.bede.org.uk/Josephus.htm (accessed April 7, 2020).

[50] Reasonable Theology, "Jesus Outside the Bible, 1—Tacitus," https://reasonabletheology.org/jesus-outside-the-bible-1-tacitus (accessed April 7, 2020).

[51] Steve Maltz, "Jesus in the Talmud," Premier, https://www.premier.org.uk/Blogs/Yeshua-Explored/Jesus-in-the-Talmud (accessed on April 7, 2020).

[52] James Rochford, "Did Jesus Exist? (Part 4: Lucian and Thallus)," Christian Apologetics Alliance, http://christianapologeticsalliance.com/2016/02/12/did-jesus-exist-part-4-lucian-and-thallus (accessed April 7, 2020).

[53] Good resources on archaeological discoveries:

- Peter Williams, "9 Archaeology Finds That Confirm the New Testament," Premier Christianity, https://www.premierchristianity.com/Past-Issues/2017/March-2017/9-archaeology-finds-that-confirm-the-New-Testament (accessed April 7, 2020).

- Peter Williams, "Archaeology and the Historical Reliability of the New Testament," Bethinking, https://www.bethinking.org/is-the-bible-reliable/archaeology-and-the-historical-reliability-of-the-new-testament (accessed April 7, 2020).

[54] Steven Bancarz, "Did Jesus Exist? All Scholars Agree He 'Certainly' Existed," Reasons for Jesus, https://reasonsforjesus.com/jesus-exist-scholars-agree-certainly-existed (accessed April 7, 2020).

[55] Amy Hall, "Where Did These Minimal Facts about the Resurrection Come From?" Stand to Reason, https://www.str.org/blog/where-did-these-minimal-facts-about-the-resurrection-come-from#.XozKJm5FzIU (accessed April 7, 2020).

[56] Matt Slick, "1 Cor. 15:3–4 Demonstrates a Creed Too Early for Legend to Corrupt," Christian Apologetics and Research Ministry, https://carm.org/1-cor-153-4-demonstrates-creed-too-early-legend-corrupt (accessed April 7, 2020).

[57] Belief Map, "Did Jesus Actually Die on the Cross?" https://beliefmap.org/jesus/die-survive/crucifixion (accessed April 7, 2020).

[58] Bart Ehrman, "Jesus' Crucifixion as King of the Jews," The Bart Ehrman Blog, https://ehrmanblog.org/jesus-crucifixion-as-king-of-the-jews (accessed on April 7, 2020).

59 Kyle Butt, "The Case of the Empty Tomb," Apologetics Press, http://www.apologeticspress.org/APContent.aspx?category=22&article=896   (accessed April 7, 2020).

60 Patton, "Eight Reasons Why the Gospels Are Embarrassing."

61 James Bishop, "The Empty Tomb Is a Historical Fact, Most Scholars Agree," Reasons for Jesus, https://reasonsforjesus.com/the-empty-tomb-is-a-historical-fact-most-scholars-agree (accessed April 7, 2020).

62 Michael Grant, *Jesus: An Historian's Review of the Gospels* (New York: Macmillan, 1992), 176.

63 "Bart Ehrman Quotes," Goodreads, https://www.goodreads.com/quotes/9652048-as-a-historian-i-am-struck-by-a-certain-consistency (accessed April 7, 2020).

64 J. Warner-Wallace, "Can Paul Actually Be Considered a Witness If He Never Actually Saw Jesus?" Cold-Case Christianity, https://coldcasechristianity.com/writings/can-paul-be-considered-a-witness-if-he-never-actually-saw-jesus (accessed April 7, 2020).

65 "Gary Habermas Quotes," Goodreads, https://www.goodreads.com/author/quotes/85706.Gary_R_Habermas (accessed April 7, 2020).

66 Laura Bailey, "Losing Hope? Have You Considered Christ?" Billy Graham Evangelistic Association. https://billygraham.org/story/losing-hope-have-you-considered-christ (accessed April 7, 2020).

67 "45 Scholar Quotes on Jesus' Resurrection Appearances," *Bishop's Encyclopedia of Religion, Society and Philosophy*, https://jamesbishopblog.com/category/world-religions (accessed April 7, 2020).

68 Rice Brooks, *God's Not Dead: Evidence for God in an Age of Uncertainty* (New York: HarperCollins, 2013), 155

69 "45 Scholar Quotes on Jesus' Resurrection Appearances."

70 "Oral Traditions," First Nations & Indigenous Studies, https://indigenousfoundations.arts.ubc.ca/oral_traditions (accessed April 8, 2020).

71 Ryan Turner, "An Analysis of the Pre-Pauline Creed in 1 Corinthians 15:1–11," Christian Apologetics and Research Ministry, https://carm.org/analysis-pre-pauline-creed-1-corinthians-151-11 (accessed April 8, 2020).

72 Belief Map, "Does Corinthians 15 Creed Date to about AD 30?" https://beliefmap.org/bible/1-corinthians/15-creed/date (accessed April 8, 2020).

73 "The Swoon Theory—What Is It? Did Jesus Survive His Crucifixion?" Compelling the Truth. https://www.compellingtruth.org/swoon-theory.html (accessed April 8, 2020).

74 Andrea Nicolotti, "What Do We Know about the Scourging of Jesus?" ASOR, http://www.asor.org/anetoday/2018/12/What-Do-We-Know-About-Scourging-Jesus (accessed April 8, 2020).

75 Gregory Lanier, "'It Was Made to Appear Like That to Them:' Islam's Denial of Jesus' Crucifixion," *Reformed Faith & Practice*, https://journal.rts.edu/article/it-was-made-to-appear-like-that-to-them-islams-denial-of-jesus-crucifixion-in-the-quran-and-dogmatic-tradition (accessed April 8, 2020).

76 William Lane-Craig, "Accounting for the Empty Tomb: The Quest for the Risen, Historical Jesus," https://www.americamagazine.org/faith/2013/03/19/accounting-empty-tomb-quest-risen-historical-jesus (accessed April 8, 2020).

77 Gary Habermas, "Explaining Away Jesus' Resurrection: Hallucination," Equip.org, https://www.equip.org/article/explaining-away-jesus-resurrection-hallucination (accessed April 8, 2020).

78 James Tabor, "Do Historians Exclude the Supernatural?" TaborBlog, https://jamestabor.com/do-historians-exclude-the-supernatural (accessed April 8, 2020).

79 Myles Munroe, "What Is Colonization?" YouTube video, 55:55, October 27, 2016, https://www.youtube.com/watch?v=yRH_BH4-Sv8.

80 Good resources on the kingdom of God:

- American Business Advisors, "Citizenship in the Kingdom of God Part I—The Kingdom, Its Government, and You." https://abadvisors.com/citizenship-in-the-kingdom-of-god-part-i-the-kingdom-its-government-and-you (accessed April 8, 2020).

- Amanda Casanova, "What Is Meant by the Kingdom of God? 10 Things to Know.," Bible Study Tools, https://www.biblestudytools.com/bible-study/explore-the-bible/what-is-meant-by-the-kingdom-of-god-10-things-to-know.html (accessed April 9, 2020).

[81] Good resources on the Beatitudes:

- "Beatitudes (Short Version)," AramaicJesus.org, http://www.aramaicjesus. org/beatitudes (accessed April 8, 2020).

- Patrician Fresen, "The Beatitudes as Translated from the Aramaic," Bridget Mary's Blog, http://bridgetmarys.blogspot.com/2017/02/the-beatitudes-as-translated-from.html (accessed April 8, 2020).

[82] Myles Munroe, "The Power of Being an Ambassador for Jesus," YouTube video, 20:48, November 6, 2016, https://www.youtube.com/watch?v=Y9VU0fWZCFY&t=797s.

[83] Richard Rohr, "What Is Contemplation?" Center for Action and Contemplation, July 1, 2020, https://cac.org/about-cac/what-is-contemplation.

[84] Douglas Bloch, *Listening to Your Inner Voice* (Center City, MN: Hazelden, 1991), 126.

[85] Anxiety and Depression Association of America, "Facts and Statistics," https://adaa.org/about-adaa/press-room/facts-statistics (accessed April 9, 2020).

[86] Scot Thomas, "Alcohol and Drug Statistics," American Addiction Centers, https://americanaddictioncenters.org/rehab-guide/addiction-statistics (accessed April 9, 2020).

[87] American Foundation for Suicide Prevention, "Suicide Statistics," https://afsp.org/about-suicide/suicide-statistics (accessed April 9, 2020).